LEARN KOTLIN

& BUILD

ANDROID APPS:

Your 30-Day Beginner's Project Guide.

Step-by-Step Guide for Mobile App

Development and Web Development."

Contents

ABOUT THE BOOK

Ever Dreamt of Building Your Own App, But Code Seems Like a Mystery or jargon?

Imagine the thrill and happiness of seeing your own creation come to life on your phone screen or any mobile screen. An app you designed, coded, and can proudly call yours. But where do you even begin and many also ask how do I even start, where do I start from?

This book is your key to unlocking the world of Android App Development, even if you're a complete beginner.

Forget dry lectures and overwhelming syntax manuals. We'll embark on a journey together, using Kotlin, a powerful yet approachable language, to build real-world projects step-by-step.

Here's what you'll achieve with this book:

Master the Fundamentals: Grasp core concepts like layouts, user interfaces, and data handling, building a strong foundation for future projects.

Project-Based Learning: No more theory overload! Learn by doing as you create engaging apps like a weather app, a to-do list, or even a simple game. Each project is meticulously explained with code examples and troubleshooting tips.

Beginner to Intermediate: Start with the basics and gradually progress to more advanced topics, ensuring a smooth learning curve that keeps you motivated.

Modern Practices: This book doesn't just teach you coding, it equips you with the latest tools and techniques used by professional developers.

Don't let the fear of the unknown hold you back. This book is written in a clear, concise, and engaging way, breaking down complex concepts into manageable steps. We'll address any roadblocks you might encounter, ensuring you have the support you need to succeed.

Ready to turn your app idea into reality? Learn Kotlin & Build Android Apps is your perfect companion on this exciting journey. It's also an amazing gift for aspiring programmers and developers who want to unlock their creative potential in the mobile app world.

PREFACE

Welcome to Learn Kotlin & Build Android Apps: Your 30-Day Beginner's Project Guide. I promise you that this will be exciting journey into Kotlin. This book is specially designed to equip you with the essential skills to start creating your own Android applications using the powerful Kotlin programming language.

What you'll learn:

Kotlin: This book introduces you to Kotlin, a modern and concise language that's specifically designed for Android development. You'll learn the fundamentals of Kotlin syntax, including all variables, data types, control flow, and functions.

Android Development Basics: We'll explore core concepts in Android development, such as activities, views, and layouts, which are the building blocks of your apps.

Project-Based Learning: This book emphasizes a practical approach. Each chapter concludes with a project or more that allows you to apply the newly acquired knowledge to build a real, functional Android app. Projects are organized to start from simple and gradually increase in complexity, giving you a clear progression as you master the skills.

Who this book is for:
 Beginners: This book is ideal for anyone with no prior programming experience who wants to learn Kotlin and develop Android apps. No prior coding knowledge is assumed.

 Experienced Developers: Even if you're familiar with other programming languages, this book can serve as a valuable introduction to Kotlin and the specific aspects of Android development.

What sets this book apart:
 Clear and Concise Explanations: We use clear and easy-to-understand language, avoiding technical jargon whenever possible. Key terms and concepts are defined within the context of the chapter, making them easier to grasp.

 Step-by-Step Approach: Each chapter is structured with a logical progression, starting with fundamental concepts and gradually building towards more complex topics.

 Emphasis on Practical Application: The project-based learning approach ensures you're not just learning theory; you're actively applying your knowledge to create real Android apps.

Why Choose Kotlin?
Many might be curious: why specifically Kotlin? With so many programming languages available, why should you choose this one for Android development? Here are your answers:

Modern and Efficient: Kotlin is a modern language designed with conciseness and expressiveness in mind. It allows you to write cleaner, more readable code compared to older languages like Java, often with fewer lines of code required to achieve the same functionality. This translates to:

i. Faster development: Spend less time writing and debugging code, allowing you to focus on bringing your app ideas to life quicker.

ii. Easier maintenance: Cleaner and more concise code is easier to understand and maintain, both for yourself and others working on the project in the future.

Seamless Integration with Android: Kotlin is officially supported by Android, meaning it integrates seamlessly with the Android development environment and tools. This ensures compatibility and a smooth development experience.

Growing Popularity: Kotlin's adoption within the Android development community is rapidly increasing. By learning Kotlin, you'll be equipped with a skill that is in high demand and will position you well for future opportunities in this growing field.

While other languages can be used for Android development, Kotlin offers a modern, efficient, and widely-adopted approach that provides significant benefits for both beginners and experienced developers.

Whether you're just starting out or looking to expand your programming skillset, Kotlin is a language worth learning for anyone interested in building the next generation of Android apps.

Chapter 1:
Welcome to Kotlin

Introduction to Kotlin Basics

Kotlin as earlier explained is a modern programming language that offers a concise and expressive syntax, making it a popular choice for Android app development and beyond. In this chapter, we'll start by having a clear understanding of the fundamental building blocks of Kotlin syntax, providing you with a solid foundation for writing Kotlin code.

Understanding Kotlin Syntax

Syntax refers to the rules and structure of a programming language, dictating how code is written and interpreted by the computer. In Kotlin, the syntax is designed to be intuitive and easy to read, allowing developers to write clean and efficient code.

Here are some key aspects of Kotlin syntax that you should be familiar with:

1. **Variables and Data Types**: In Kotlin, variables are used to store data values, and each variable has a specific data type that defines the kind of data it can hold. Common data types in Kotlin include integers, floating-point numbers, booleans, and strings.

Example:

```kotlin
val number: Int = 10
val name: String = "John"
```

2. **Functions**: Functions are blocks of code that perform a specific task or operation. In Kotlin, functions are defined using the `fun` keyword, followed by the function name and parameters (if any). Functions can also return values using the `return` keyword.

Example:

```kotlin
fun add(a: Int, b: Int): Int {

    return a + b

}
```

3. **Control Flow Statements**: Control flow statements allow you to control the flow of execution in your code, based on certain conditions. In Kotlin, you can use if-else statements, when expressions, and loops (such as `for` and `while`) to control the flow of your program.

Example:

```kotlin
val x = 10
if (x > 0) {

    println("Positive number")

} else {

    println("Negative number")

}
```

```
```

Variables:

A variable is a named storage location in a program's memory where data can be stored and manipulated. Think of it as a container that holds a value, which can change over the course of a program's execution. In Kotlin, variables are declared using the `val` or `var` keywords.

- `val`: Declares an immutable variable, meaning its value cannot be changed once it's assigned.
- `var`: Declares a mutable variable, allowing its value to be modified as needed.

For example:

```kotlin
val pi = 3.14 // Declares an immutable variable 'pi' with the value 3.14

var count = 0 // Declares a mutable variable 'count' with the initial value of 0
```

Data Types:

Every value in Kotlin has a specific data type, which determines the kind of data that can be stored in a variable and the operations that can be performed on it. Kotlin provides a rich set of data types, including:

1. Numeric Data Types:

   - `Int`: Represents whole numbers (e.g., 5, -10, 100).

   - `Double`: Represents double-precision floating-point numbers (e.g., 3.14, -0.5, 10.0).

   - `Float`: Represents single-precision floating-point numbers (e.g., 3.14f, -0.5f, 10.0f).

   - `Long`: Represents long integers (e.g., 100L, -200L).

2. Boolean Data Type:

   - `Boolean`: Represents a value that can be either `true` or `false`.

3. Character Data Type:

   - `Char`: Represents a single Unicode character (e.g., 'a', 'B', '@').

4. String Data Type:

   - `String`: Represents a sequence of characters (e.g., "Hello", "Kotlin", "123").

For example:

```kotlin
val age: Int = 25 // Declares an integer variable 'age' with the value 25
```

```kotlin
val pi: Double = 3.14 // Declares a double variable 'pi' with the value 3.14

val isKotlinFun: Boolean = true // Declares a boolean variable 'isKotlinFun' with the value true

val firstLetter: Char = 'A' // Declares a char variable 'firstLetter' with the value 'A'

val greeting: String = "Hello, Kotlin!" // Declares a string variable 'greeting' with the value "Hello, Kotlin!"
```

What is a Function?

A function is a block of code that performs a specific task. It takes input, processes it, and produces output. Functions are essential building blocks of any programming language, allowing developers to break down complex tasks into smaller, more manageable pieces.

In Kotlin, functions are declared using the `fun` keyword, followed by the function name and optional parameters. Here's a basic example of a Kotlin function:

```kotlin
fun greet(name: String) {
    println("Hello, $name!")
}
```

In the above example, `greet` is the function name, and `name` is a parameter of type `String`. The function prints a greeting message to the console, using the value of the `name` parameter.

Function Parameters

Parameters are variables that are passed to a function when it is called. They provide input to the function, allowing it to perform its task with different values. In Kotlin, parameters are declared within parentheses after the function name. Multiple parameters can be separated by commas.

```kotlin
fun add(a: Int, b: Int): Int {

    return a + b

}
```

In this example, the `add` function takes two parameters (`a` and `b`) of type `Int` and returns their sum as an `Int`.

Return Types

The return type of a function specifies the type of value it returns after performing its task. In Kotlin, the return type is declared after a colon (`:`) following the parameter list. If a function does not return any value, its return type is specified as `Unit`, which is equivalent to `void` in other programming languages.

```kotlin
```

```
fun multiply(x: Int, y: Int): Int {

    return x  y

}
```
```

In this example, the `multiply` function takes two parameters (`x` and `y`) of type `Int` and returns their product as an `Int`.


## Calling Functions

To use a function in Kotlin, you simply call it by its name and provide the required arguments, if any. Here's how you can call the `greet` function defined earlier:


```kotlin
greet("John")
```
```

This will print "Hello, John!" to the console.

1.1: Setting Up Your Development Environment

Setting Up Your Toolkit

Here's what you need to do:

1. **Download and Install Android Studio:**

Android Studio is the official integrated development environment (IDE) for building Android apps. An IDE is like a comprehensive workbench that combines tools for writing code, editing, debugging, and running your applications.

You can download Android Studio for free from the official website: https://developer.android.com/studio

Once downloaded, follow the on-screen instructions to install it on your computer.

2. **Configure Your Emulator or Connect a Device:**

An emulator is a software program that simulates a physical Android device on your computer. This allows you to test and run your apps without needing an actual device.

Alternatively, you can connect a physical Android device to your computer using a USB cable. This can be helpful for testing how your app behaves on real hardware.

Android Studio provides options to both create and manage emulators and connect physical devices. Refer to the official documentation for detailed instructions:

https://developer.android.com/studio/install

3. **Explore the Interface:**

 Once you have Android Studio installed and configured, take some time to familiarize yourself with the interface.

 The interface consists of different panels and windows that you'll use throughout the development process.

 Don't worry about memorizing everything at once. As you progress through the book, you'll naturally learn about the different functionalities and how to use them effectively.

Don't hesitate to consult the official Android Studio documentation or online tutorials if you encounter any difficulties during the setup process. There are many resources available to help you get started.

1.2: Your First Kotlin Program: Hello, World

Every programmer's journey begins with a simple yet significant milestone: printing "Hello, World!" to the screen. In this very chapter, you'll write your very first Kotlin program and explore fundamental elements like variables, data types, and printing statements.

1.2.1: Creating Your Program:

1. Open Android Studio: Launch the Android Studio software you installed earlier.

2. Start a New Project: Click on "Start a new Android Studio project" and follow the on-screen instructions to create a new project. You can choose a simple name like "HelloWorldApp" for your project.

3. Locate the Kotlin File: Once the project is created, navigate to the "app" folder within your project directory. You should see a file named "MainActivity.kt". This is the Kotlin file where you'll write your code.

1.2.2: Writing Your First Lines:

1. Open the "MainActivity.kt" file: Double-click on the "MainActivity.kt" file to open it in the code editor.

2. Add the "fun main" Function: Every Kotlin program needs a starting point, which is defined by a function named main. This function tells the program where to begin execution. Type the following line of code inside the curly braces of the "main" function:

```kotlin
println("Hello, World!")
```

Notes

 println: This is a built-in function in Kotlin that allows you to print a message to the console.

"Hello, World!": This is the text you want to print, enclosed within double quotes ("").

1.2.3: Running the Program:

1. Run the App: Click the green "Run" button (play button triangle) in the top toolbar of Android Studio.

2. Observe the Output: If everything is set up correctly, you should see a new window appear titled "Run app" with the message "Hello, World!" printed within it.

If you followed the above steps and instructions carefully, congratulations! You've successfully written and run your first Kotlin program.

1.2.4: Understanding the Basics:

This simple program introduces you to a few fundamental concepts:

Variables: While not explicitly used in this example, variables are used to store and manipulate data within your program. You'll learn more about them in later chapters.

Data Types: In "Hello, World!", the text "Hello, World!" is considered a String data type, which represents textual data.

Printing Statements: The `println` function is an example of a printing statement, which allows you to display information on the console.

1.3: Project 1: Building a Greeting App

Variables: These are like containers that store information you can use in your program. Think of them like labels attached to boxes holding specific pieces of data.

User Input: This refers to how your app collects information from the user, such as their name in this case.

String Manipulation: This involves working with text data, like combining strings or extracting specific characters.

Steps:

1. Start a New Android Studio Project:

Open Android Studio and start a new project. Choose a suitable name for your app (e.g., "GreetingApp") and select "Empty Activity" as the template. Click "Finish" to create the project.

2. Modify the Activity Layout:

In the Project pane on the left, navigate to the app > res > layout folder. This folder contains files defining the visual structure of your app's screens.

Open the file named activity_main.xml in the layout editor. This file represents the layout of your main screen.

In the layout editor, drag and drop a TextView element from the palette onto the design surface. A TextView displays text to the user.

Change the text displayed in the TextView by clicking its properties panel and modifying the "text" attribute. You can write something like "Enter your name:" here.

Below the TextView, drag and drop an EditText element. This allows users to type in their name.

Modify the "hint" attribute of the EditText to provide a hint for the user, like "e.g., John Doe".

3. Write the Code to Handle User Input and Display Greeting:

In the Project pane, navigate to the app > java > [your package name] folder (e.g., "app > java > com.example.greetingapp").

Open the MainActivity.kt file. This file contains the code that controls the behavior of your app's main screen.

Locate the onCreate function within this file. This function is called when your app's main activity is first created.

Inside the onCreate function, add the following code:

```kotlin
// 1. Declare a variable to store the user's name
var name: String = ""


// 2. Find the EditText and TextView elements using their IDs
val inputName = findViewById<EditText>(R.id.name_input) // Replace "name_input" with the actual ID from your layout
val greetingText = findViewById<TextView>(R.id.greeting_text) // Replace "greeting_text" with the actual ID from your layout


// 3. Add a button click listener
val button = findViewById<Button>(R.id.greet_button) // Replace "greet_button" with the actual ID from your layout
button.setOnClickListener {
    // 4. Get the user's input from the EditText
    name = inputName.text.toString()


    // 5. Construct the greeting message
    val greeting = "Hello, $name! Welcome to our app."
```

```
// 6. Update the TextView with the greeting message

    greetingText.text = greeting

}
```

Explanation:

Line 1: We declare a variable named "name" of type "String" to store the user's name. Think of it as a box labeled "name" that can hold text data.

Lines 2-3: We use the `findViewById` method to find the EditText and TextView elements from the layout file and store them in variables. This allows us to interact with these elements in our code.

Lines 4-6: We add a click listener to the button element. When the user clicks the button, the code within the curly braces will be executed.

Line 5: We retrieve the text the user entered in the EditText using the `text` property and convert it to a string using `toString()`. We then store it in the "name" variable.

Line 6: We construct a greeting message by combining the retrieved name with a string using string concatenation (joining strings).

Line 7: We update the text displayed in the TextView by setting its "text" property to the constructed greeting message.

4. Run the App:

Click the "Run" button (green triangle) in the toolbar.

Select your preferred device or create a new emulator.

Chapter 2:
Deeper into Kotlin Fundamentals

Reading User Input

User input is any information provided by the user to the program during its execution. This input can come from various sources, such as keyboard input, touchscreen interactions, or voice commands. In Kotlin, we can read user input using the `readLine()` function, which reads a line of text entered by the user from the console.

Example:

```kotlin
fun main() {
    print("Enter your name: ")
    val name = readLine()
    println("Hello, $name!")
}
```

In this example, the `readLine()` function is used to read the user's input, which is then stored in the variable `name`. We can then use this input to customize the program's output.

Outputting Results

Outputting results refers to displaying information or data generated by the program to the user. In Kotlin, we use the `println()` function to print a line of text to the console. This function adds a newline character after the text, ensuring that each output appears on a separate line.

Example:

```kotlin
fun main() {

    val message = "Welcome to Kotlin programming!"

    println(message)

}
```

In this example, the `println()` function is used to output the message "Welcome to Kotlin programming!" to the console.

Formatting Output in Kotlin

Formatting output involves arranging and presenting data in a specific format for better readability or aesthetic appeal. In Kotlin, we can use string templates to format output dynamically by embedding expressions within string literals.

Example:

```kotlin
fun main() {
    val name = "John"
    val age = 30
    println("Name: $name, Age: $age")
}
```

In this example, string interpolation is used to insert the values of variables `name` and `age` into the output string, resulting in the formatted output "Name: John, Age: 30".

By mastering these concepts, you'll be equipped to handle user input and output effectively in your Kotlin programs. These skills are essential for creating interactive and user-friendly applications. In the next chapter, we'll explore more advanced topics in Kotlin programming.

2.1: Control Flow Statements: Making Decisions

In any program, control flow refers to the order in which instructions are executed. Up until now, we've seen code executed sequentially, one line after another. However, real-world applications often need to make decisions and respond based on different conditions. This is where control flow statements come into play.

This very chapter introduces conditional statements, specifically the "if" and "else" statements, which are fundamental tools for controlling the flow of your program. They allow you to execute different instructions based on whether a certain condition is true or false.

In programming, control flow refers to the order in which your code gets executed. Sometimes, you might want your program to behave differently based on certain conditions. This is where control flow statements come in!

Think of control flow statements like decision-making tools for your program. They allow you to:

Check if a condition is true or false.

Execute different parts of your code based on the outcome of the condition.

One of the most fundamental control flow statements is the "if" statement. It allows you to specify a condition and a block of code to execute if that condition is true.

Here's the basic structure of an "if" statement in Kotlin:

```kotlin
if (condition) {
    // Code to execute if the condition is true
```

```
}
```

For example, let's say you want to write a program that checks if a user is older than 18 and displays a message accordingly. Here's how you could do it:

```kotlin
val age = 25


if (age >= 18) {

    println("You are eligible to vote.")

}
```

NOTE

`val age = 25` defines a variable named `age` and assigns it the value 25.

`if (age >= 18)` checks the condition if `age` is greater than or equal to 18.

`println("You are eligible to vote.")` is the code that gets executed only if the condition is true (i.e., if the user's age is 18 or older).

The "else" statement is another important control flow statement. It allows you to specify an alternative block of code to execute if the condition in the `if` statement is not true.

Here's the basic structure of an "if-else" statement:

```kotlin
if (condition) {
    // Code to execute if the condition is true
} else {
    // Code to execute if the condition is false
}
```

Using the same example, you can modify the code to include an `else` statement to display a different message if the user is not eligible to vote:

```kotlin
val age = 25

if (age >= 18) {
    println("You are eligible to vote.")
} else {
```

```kotlin
    println("You are not eligible to vote.")

}
```

By combining `if` and `else` statements, you can create more complex decision-making logic in your programs.

Imagine you have a door locked with a key. You only want to open the door (execute a certain part of your code) if you have the correct key (the condition is true). This is another place the `if` statement shines!

The `if` statement allows you to specify a condition. If that condition is true, a block of code following the `if` statement will be executed.

If the condition is false, an optional `else` block can be used to execute a different set of code.

```kotlin
if (condition) {

    // Code to execute if the condition is true

} else {

    // Code to execute if the conditio

n is false (optional)

}
```

Combining Conditions with Logical Operators

Imagine you have two locks on your treasure chest, and both need keys to open. This is where logical operators come in handy! They allow you to combine multiple conditions.

`&&` (AND): Both conditions must be true for the combined condition to be true.

`||` (OR): As long as at least one condition is true, the combined condition is true.

Here's an example on how to use the `AND` operator:

```kotlin
var hasPermission = true
var isQualified = true


if (hasPermission && isQualified) {
    println("You are eligible to proceed.")
} else {
    println("You are not eligible to proceed.")
}
```

In this example, both `hasPermission` and `isQualified` need to be true for the user to be eligible. If either condition is false, the user is not eligible.

Logical operators allow you to create more complex decision-making logic in your programs.

2.2: Loops: Repeating Tasks Efficiently

Imagine you need to perform a task repeatedly, like printing the same message ten times or checking ten items in a list. Writing the code for each repetition individually would be tedious and inefficient. This is where loops come into place.

Loops are a programming construct that allows you to automate repetitive tasks. They execute a block of code multiple times, based on a certain condition.

There are two main types of loops we'll focus on:

1. "for" loops:

 Purpose: Ideal when you know the exact number of times you want to repeat the code block.

 How it works:

   You define a starting value, an ending value, and an increment/decrement step for a counter variable.

The loop continues to execute the code block as long as the counter variable is within the specified range.

After each iteration (execution), the counter variable is automatically updated based on the step value.

2. "while" loops:

Purpose: Useful when you don't know beforehand how many times you need to repeat the code block, but you have a condition that determines when to stop.

How it works:

You define a condition that needs to be true for the loop to continue.

The loop executes the code block as long as the condition remains true.

Inside the loop, you typically modify the condition or variables that affect the condition to eventually make it false, causing the loop to terminate.

Choosing the right loop type:

Use a "for" loop if you know the exact number of repetitions needed.

Use a "while" loop if the number of repetitions is unknown or depends on a condition.

Example:

Here's a simple example using both "for" and "while" loops to print the numbers from 1 to 5:

```kotlin
// Using a "for" loop
for (i in 1..5) {
    println(i)
}


// Using a "while" loop
var counter = 1
while (counter <= 5) {
    println(counter)
    counter++ // Increment counter after each iteration
}
```

By understanding and using loops effectively, you can write cleaner, more concise, and efficient code, especially when dealing with repetitive tasks in your Android apps.

While "for" and "while" loops are the most common, there are a few additional loop variations you might encounter:

1. "do-while" loop:

Similar to a "while" loop, but the code block is guaranteed to execute at least once, even if the condition is initially false.

This can be helpful when you need to perform an action at least once before checking the condition to continue further iterations.

2. "for-each" loop:

A concise way to iterate over elements in a collection (like a list or array).

Instead of manually managing a counter variable, the loop automatically iterates through each element in the collection, assigning it to a temporary variable within the code block.

3. Nested loops:

Loops can be nested inside other loops, creating a hierarchy of repeated execution.

This can be useful for tasks involving multiple levels of repetition, like iterating through rows and columns in a 2D array.

Choosing the appropriate loop type depends on the specific needs of your code:

Clarity: Choose the loop type that makes your code easier to understand and maintain.

Efficiency: Consider the performance implications of different loop types, especially when dealing with large datasets.

Readability: Strive for concise and readable code, avoiding unnecessarily complex loop structures.

Mastering loops is essential for writing efficient and well-structured code in various programming domains, including Android development. As you progress through the book and projects, you'll encounter various practical scenarios where applying the right loop type will be crucial for building your apps effectively.

2.3: Project 2: Creating a Quiz Game

Let's Put your newfound skills in conditional statements, loops, and user input to the test by creating a simple quiz game!

Functionality:

The game will present multiple-choice questions to the user.

The user will select an answer from the provided options.

The game will check the user's answer against the correct answer and provide feedback.

The game will keep track of the score and display it to the user.

Steps:

1. Design the Quiz:

Decide on the topic of your quiz and prepare several questions with corresponding answer choices.

Define the correct answer for each question.

Consider including different difficulty levels for the questions (optional).

2. Implement the Logic:

Use "if" statements to check if the user's chosen answer matches the correct answer.

Use a "while" loop to keep presenting questions and checking answers until the quiz ends (e.g., after a set number of questions).

Utilize variables to store the user's score and update it based on correct answers.

3. Build the User Interface:

Design the user interface using Android Studio's layout editor.

Use TextViews to display the questions, answer options, and feedback messages.

Use Buttons or other input elements for users to select their answers.

Display the current score using a TextView.

Tips:

Start with a small number of questions to test your logic and user interface.

Gradually increase the complexity as you gain confidence.

You can add visual elements like images or sound effects to enhance the user experience (optional).

Steps:

1. Setting Up the Quiz Data:

Define an array of questions, where each question is an object containing the following properties:

`question`: The actual question text.

`options`: An array of strings representing the multiple-choice options.

`answer`: The index of the correct answer within the `options` array (starting from 0).

```kotlin
val questions = arrayOf(

    Question("What is the capital of England?", arrayOf("London", "Paris", "Berlin"), 1),

    Question("What is the largest planet in our solar system?", arrayOf("Earth", "Mars", "Jupiter"), 2),

    Question("What year did the first iPhone launch?", arrayOf("2004", "2007", "2010"), 1)

)
```

2. Implementing the Game Logic:

Use a loop to iterate through each question in the `questions` array.

Inside the loop:

Display the current question to the user using `println` or a dedicated TextView in your Android app.

Use a loop to iterate through the `options` array and display each option to the user, allowing them to choose an answer (e.g., using buttons or text input).

Get the user's answer (e.g., reading user input from an EditText field).

Compare the user's answer index with the correct answer index stored in the question object.

If the answers match, update the score and display feedback like "Correct!".

Otherwise, display feedback like "Incorrect. The correct answer is [correct answer]".

3. Displaying the Result:

After iterating through all questions, display the final score to the user using `println` or a dedicated TextView.

Here's an example code snippet illustrating the basic logic:

```kotlin
var score = 0

for (question in questions) {
    println(question.question)
    for (i in question.options.indices) {
        println("${i + 1}. ${question.options[i]}")
    }

    val userAnswer = readLine()?.toIntOrNull() ?: -1 // Handle invalid input

    if (userAnswer == question.answer) {
        score++
        println("Correct!")
    } else {
        println("Incorrect. The correct answer is ${question.options[question.answer]}.")
    }
}
```

```
println("Your final score is: $score out of ${questions.size}")
```
```

This is a simplified example for learning purposes.

In a real Android app, you would utilize appropriate UI components like TextViews, Buttons, and potentially layouts to create a user-friendly interface for interacting with the quiz.

You can further enhance the game by:

Randomizing the order of answer options.

Adding a timer for each question.

Implementing different difficulty levels.
```

Alternative 2

Step 1: Setting Up Your Project

1. Open Android Studio and create a new project.

2. Choose a project name and select "Empty Activity" as the template.

3. Follow the prompts to set up your project, including choosing a package name and selecting your target API level.

Step 2: Designing the User Interface

1. Open the activity_main.xml layout file.

2. Design the layout to include TextViews for displaying questions and options, and Buttons for selecting answers and navigating through the quiz.

Step 3: Writing Kotlin Code

1. Open the MainActivity.kt file.

2. Declare variables to store the questions, options, correct answers, and user's score:

   ```kotlin
   ```

```kotlin
private val questions = listOf(
    "What is the capital of France?",
    "Which planet is closest to the sun?",
    // Add more questions as needed
)


private val options = listOf(
    listOf("Paris", "Berlin", "Rome", "Madrid"),
    listOf("Venus", "Mercury", "Earth", "Mars"),
    // Add more options for each question
)


private val correctAnswers = listOf(0, 1, / Add correct answer indices /)


private var currentQuestionIndex = 0
private var score = 0
```

Step 4: Displaying Questions and Options

1. Create a function to display the current question and options:

```kotlin
private fun displayQuestion() {

    val                    questionTextView                    =
findViewById<TextView>(R.id.questionTextView)
    val                    optionsRadioGroup                   =
findViewById<RadioGroup>(R.id.optionsRadioGroup)


    questionTextView.text = questions[currentQuestionIndex]


    options[currentQuestionIndex].forEachIndexed { index, option ->
        val radioButton = RadioButton(this)
        radioButton.text = option
        optionsRadioGroup.addView(radioButton)
    }
}
```

Step 5: Checking User's Answer

1. Add a function to check the user's selected answer:

```kotlin
private fun checkAnswer() {

    val selectedRadioButtonId =
optionsRadioGroup.checkedRadioButtonId

    val userAnswerIndex =
optionsRadioGroup.indexOfChild(findViewById(selectedRadioButto
nId))


    if (userAnswerIndex == correctAnswers[currentQuestionIndex])
{

        score++

    }

}
```

Step 6: Handling Next Button Click

1. Implement functionality for the "Next" button to move to the next question:

```kotlin
```

```kotlin
private fun setupNextButton() {
    val nextButton = findViewById<Button>(R.id.nextButton)
    nextButton.setOnClickListener {
        checkAnswer()
        currentQuestionIndex++
        if (currentQuestionIndex < questions.size) {
            displayQuestion()
        } else {
            showScore()
        }
    }
}
```

Step 7: Displaying Final Score

1. Create a function to display the final score once all questions have been answered:

```kotlin
private fun showScore() {
```

```
    val                    scoreTextView                    =
findViewById<TextView>(R.id.scoreTextView)

    scoreTextView.text = "Your Score: $score / ${questions.size}"

}
```

Step 8: Testing Your App

1. Run your app on an emulator or physical device.

2. Go through the quiz, selecting answers for each question.

3. Observe the score displayed at the end of the quiz.

Bonus

Adding a Timer to the Quiz Game

Here's how you can enhance the quiz game from Project 2 by adding a timer for each question:

1. Importing the Timer Class:

First, you need to import the `Timer` class from the `java.util` package. This class provides functionality for creating and managing timed events.

```kotlin
import java.util.Timer

TimerTask
```

2. Creating the Timer Function:

Define a separate function to handle the timer functionality for each question. This function will take the following arguments:

 questionDuration: The duration of the timer in seconds.

 onTick: An optional callback function to be executed periodically (every second in this case).

 onFinish: A callback function to be executed when the timer finishes.

```kotlin
fun startTimer(questionDuration: Int, onTick: (() -> Unit)? = null,
onFinish: () -> Unit) {

    val timer = Timer()

    val timerTask = object : TimerTask() {

        override fun run() {

            // Update UI or perform actions for each tick (optional)

            onTick?.invoke()

        }

    }


    timer.schedule(timerTask, 0, 1000) // Schedule the task with initial
delay 0 and interval 1000ms (1 second)


    timer.schedule(object : TimerTask() {

        override fun run() {

            timer.cancel()  // Cancel the timer after questionDuration
seconds

            onFinish.invoke()

        }

    }, questionDuration    1000) // Schedule timer completion after
questionDuration seconds
```

```
}
```
```

Explanation:

The `startTimer` function accepts three arguments:

`questionDuration`: Defines the timer duration in seconds.

`onTick`: An optional callback function that can be used to update the UI or perform actions every second during the timer duration.

`onFinish`: A callback function that gets executed when the timer finishes (after `questionDuration` seconds).

Inside the function:

A `Timer` object is created.

A `TimerTask` is defined to handle the timer's behavior.

The `run` method of the `TimerTask` is called every second (defined by the `schedule` method with an interval of 1000 milliseconds).

The optional `onTick` callback can be used here to update the UI (e.g., displaying a countdown timer) or perform other actions each second.

Another `TimerTask` is scheduled to run after the specified `questionDuration` in milliseconds.

This `TimerTask` cancels the timer and calls the `onFinish` callback, signaling the end of the question timer.
```

3. Integrating the Timer in the Quiz Loop:

Modify the quiz loop in Project 2 to integrate the timer function:

```kotlin
for (question in questions) {
    println(question.question)

    startTimer(10) { // Set timer duration to 10 seconds
        println("Time remaining: ${10 - it} seconds") // Update countdown timer (example)
    } onFinish {
        // Handle end of timer (e.g., disable answer input, move to next question)
    }

    for (i in question.options.indices) {
        println("${i + 1}. ${question.options[i]}")
    }

    // ... remaining quiz logic (get user answer, check answer, etc.)
}
```

In the quiz loop, call the `startTimer` function before displaying the answer options.

Pass the desired timer duration (e.g., 10 seconds) as the first argument.

The optional `onTick` callback can be used to update the UI, like displaying a countdown timer showing the remaining seconds. Update the displayed time within the callback (example: "Time remaining: ${10 - it} seconds").

The `onFinish` callback can be used to handle actions when the timer finishes, such as disabling user input for the question, moving to the next question, or displaying a message indicating time is up.

In a real Android app, you'll need to use appropriate UI elements like TextViews or ProgressBars to visually represent the timer and update it dynamically based on the `onTick` callback.

You can adjust the timer duration and customize the behavior within the `onTick` and `onFinish` callbacks to suit your specific game design.

Chapter 3:
Working with Numbers and Expressions

3.1: Understanding Different Number Types

In programming, numbers play a crucial role in representing various quantities, measurements, and calculations. Kotlin provides different number types to handle these values effectively.

1. Integers: Represent whole numbers without decimal points, like 10, -5, or 1234.

 They are typically used for counting, indexing, or representing whole units.

 In Kotlin, integers are declared using the `Int` type.

Example:
```kotlin
val age = 25

val score = 100

val numberOfItems = 5
```

2. Doubles:

Represent floating-point numbers with a decimal part, like 3.14, -12.56, or 1.0.

They are used for precise calculations involving decimals, such as scientific calculations, measurements, or financial values.

In Kotlin, doubles are declared using the `Double` type.

Example:

```kotlin
val pi = 3.14159
val averageScore = 87.5
val price = 9.99
```

3. Floats:

Similar to doubles, they represent floating-point numbers with decimals.

However, floats offer less precision than doubles (typically 6-7 decimal places compared to 15-16 for doubles).

They are used when you need to save memory or when the full precision of a double is not essential.

In Kotlin, floats are declared using the `Float` type.

Example:

```kotlin
val temperature = 25.5f // 'f' suffix indicates a float literal
val distance = 1000.0f // Can also use a decimal without a suffix
```

Choosing the right number type:

Use `Int` for whole numbers where decimal precision is not required.

Use `Double` for calculations involving decimals and high precision is essential.

Use `Float` when memory efficiency is a concern and slightly less precision is acceptable.

Understanding Type Conversion and Casting in Kotlin

In programming, different data types exist to represent various kinds of information, like numbers, text, and booleans. When working with these data types, you might encounter situations where you need to convert a value from one type to another. This process is called type conversion or casting.

Data types: Define the category and properties of data your program can handle. Examples include integers (whole numbers), floating-point numbers (numbers with decimals), and strings (text).

Type conversion: The process of transforming a value from one data type to another.

Casting: A specific type of conversion where you explicitly instruct the program to treat a value as a different data type.

Understanding the need for type conversion:

Imagine you have an `Int` variable storing a score (100 points) and want to display it as a percentage (100.0%). Since `Int` cannot hold decimals, you'll need to convert the score to a `Double` (floating-point number) to represent the percentage accurately.

Type conversion in Kotlin:

Unlike some other languages, Kotlin does not allow implicit type conversion from smaller data types (like `Byte`, `Short`, `Int`) to larger ones (like `Long`, `Float`, `Double`). This is a deliberate design choice to prevent potential errors and ensure type safety.

However, Kotlin provides explicit conversion functions for safe and controlled type conversion. These functions have names like `toByte()`, `toInt()`, `toLong()`, `toFloat()`, and `toDouble()`, depending on the target data type.

Example:

```kotlin
val score: Int = 100
```

```kotlin
val percentage: Double = score.toDouble() // Explicit conversion using toDouble()

println("Score: $score, Percentage: $percentage%")
```

Casting in Kotlin:

While discouraged in most cases due to potential data loss or unexpected behavior, Kotlin allows casting using the `as` keyword. Casting essentially tells the compiler to treat a value as a specific type, but it's crucial to be cautious and ensure the conversion is valid.

Example:
```kotlin
val largeNumber: Long = 1234567890L

val smallerNumber: Int = largeNumber as Int // Casting using 'as' keyword

println("Large number: $largeNumber, Smaller number (casted): $smallerNumber")
```

 Explicit conversion functions are generally preferred over casting due to better type safety and clarity.

Casting can lead to data loss if the source value cannot be accurately represented in the target type.

Always exercise caution when using casting and consider potential consequences before employing it.

3.2: Operators and Expressions: Performing Calculations

In any programming language, operators are symbols that perform operations on values. They allow you to manipulate data and create expressions to perform calculations.

3.2.1: Mathematical Operators:

Kotlin provides a variety of mathematical operators for performing common calculations:

Arithmetic operators:

`+`: Addition

`-`: Subtraction

``: Multiplication

`/`: Division

`%`: Modulo (remainder after division)

Increment (++) and decrement (--) operators:

These operators are used to increase or decrease the value of a variable by 1.

They can be used in two ways:

`++variable`: Pre-increment (increment and then use the value)

`variable++`: Post-increment (use the value and then increment)

Decrement operators (--) work similarly.

Examples:

```kotlin
val num1 = 10
val num2 = 5

val sum = num1 + num2 // sum will be 15
val difference = num1 - num2 // difference will be 5
val product = num1  num2 // product will be 50
val remainder = num1 % num2 // remainder will be 0

var count = 0
```

```
count++ // count becomes 1 (post-increment)

++count // count becomes 2 (pre-increment)

```

3.2.2: Combining Operators and Variables:

You can combine operators and variables to create complex expressions. Remember the order of operations (PEMDAS: Parentheses, Exponents, Multiplication and Division from left to right, Addition and Subtraction from left to right) to ensure the calculations are performed correctly.

Example:

```kotlin
val area = (length  width) / 2 // Calculates the area of a triangle

```

3.2.3: Understanding Operator Precedence:

When multiple operators are present in an expression, they are evaluated according to their precedence. Operators with higher precedence are evaluated first. If operators have the same precedence, they are evaluated from left to right.

Example:

```kotlin

val result = 2 + 3  4 // Evaluates to 14, not 20

// Multiplication (higher precedence) is performed first (3  4 = 12), then addition (2 + 12 = 14)

```

3.2.4: Additional Operators:

Comparison operators:

  `==`: Equal to

  `!=`: Not equal to

  `<`: Less than

  `>`: Greater than

  `<=`: Less than or equal to

  `>=`: Greater than or equal to

Logical operators:

  `&&`: AND (both conditions must be true)

  `||`: OR (at least one condition must be true)

  `!`: NOT (inverts the truth value)

Assignment operators:

`=`: Simple assignment

`+=`, `-=`, `=`, `/=`, etc.: Combine assignment and operation (e.g., `x += 5` is equivalent to `x = x + 5`)

Bitwise operators:

Used for manipulating bits within numbers (less common for most beginner Android development tasks)

Type Casting:

Sometimes, you might need to convert a value from one data type to another. Kotlin provides type casting using the `as` keyword or casting functions like `toInt()`, `toDouble()`, etc.

Example:

```kotlin
val age = "25" as Int // Converts the string "25" to an integer (age will
be 25)
```

Be cautious when using type casting, as it can lead to errors if the conversion is not possible.

Always ensure the data type you're casting to is compatible with the original value.

3.3: Project 3: Building a Simple Calculator App

3.3: Project 3: Building a Simple Calculator App

Challenge yourself by creating a basic calculator app using Kotlin! This project will solidify your understanding of number types, operators, user input, and how to combine them to build a functional application.

Functionality:

 The calculator will allow users to enter two numbers.

 It will provide buttons or functionalities to perform basic arithmetic operations like addition, subtraction, multiplication, and division.

 The app will display the calculated result based on the chosen operation.

Steps:

1. Setting Up the User Interface:

While this example focuses on the logic, you can create a simple user interface (UI) in Android Studio using various UI components like buttons and text fields. However, for this demonstration, we'll use basic console input and output for simplicity.

2. Declaring Variables:

Define variables to store the two numbers entered by the user:

```kotlin
var num1: Double = 0.0
var num2: Double = 0.0
```

We use `Double` data type to handle both whole numbers and decimals.

3. Getting User Input:

Use the `readLine()` function to read user input from the console:

```kotlin
println("Enter the first number:")
```

```
num1 = readLine()?.toDoubleOrNull() ?: 0.0 // Handle invalid input

println("Enter the second number:")
num2 = readLine()?.toDoubleOrNull() ?: 0.0
```

`readLine()` reads the user's input as a string.

`toDoubleOrNull()` attempts to convert the string to a double, returning null if the conversion fails.

The `?:` operator (Elvis operator) assigns a default value (0.0 in this case) if the conversion result is null (invalid input).

4. Implementing Calculations:

Define functions for each arithmetic operation:

```kotlin
fun add(x: Double, y: Double): Double {
    return x + y
}
```

```
fun subtract(x: Double, y: Double): Double {

    return x - y

}


fun multiply(x: Double, y: Double): Double {

    return x  y

}


fun divide(x: Double, y: Double): Double {

    if (y == 0.0) {

        println("Error: Division by zero is not allowed.")

        return 0.0 // Handle division by zero error

    } else {

        return x / y

    }

}
```
```

Each function takes two double arguments and returns the calculated result.
```

The `divide` function includes an error check to prevent division by zero and displays an appropriate message.

5. Choosing the Operation:

Prompt the user to choose the desired operation:

```kotlin
println("Choose an operation:")
println("1. Add")
println("2. Subtract")
println("3. Multiply")
println("4. Divide")

val choice = readLine()?.toIntOrNull() ?: 0 // Handle invalid input
```

Use a `when` expression to perform the calculation based on the user's choice:

```kotlin
```

```kotlin
val result = when (choice) {
    1 -> add(num1, num2)
    2 -> subtract(num1, num2)
    3 -> multiply(num1, num2)
    4 -> divide(num1, num2)
    else -> {
        println("Invalid choice.")
        0.0 // Default value in case of invalid choice
    }
}
```

The `when` expression evaluates the `choice` variable and executes the corresponding code block for each valid option.

6. Displaying the Result:

Print the calculated result to the console:

```kotlin
println("The result is: $result")
```

Complete code example:

```kotlin
fun main() {
    var num1: Double = 0.0
    var num2: Double = 0.0

    println("Enter the first number:")
    num1 = readLine()?.toDoubleOrNull() ?: 0.0

    println("Enter the second number:")
    num2 = readLine()?.toDoubleOrNull() ?: 0.0

    println("Choose an operation:")
    println("1. Add")
    println("2. Subtract")
    println("3. Multiply")
    println("4. Divide")

    val choice = readLine()?.toIntOrNull() ?: 0
```

```kotlin
val result = when (choice) {
    1 -> add(num1, num2)
    2 -> subtract(num1, num2)
    3 -> multiply(num1, num2)
    4 -> divide(num1, num2)
```

Alternative 2

Step 1: Setting Up Your Project

1. Open Android Studio and create a new project.

2. Choose a project name and select "Empty Activity" as the template.

3. Follow the prompts to set up your project, including choosing a package name and selecting your target API level.

Step 2: Designing the User Interface

1. Open the activity_main.xml layout file.

2. Design the layout to include TextViews for displaying the numbers and result, and Buttons for inputting numbers and operators.

Step 3: Writing Kotlin Code

1. Open the MainActivity.kt file.

2. Declare variables to store the current calculation expression and result:

```kotlin
private var currentExpression = ""
private var currentResult = 0.0
```

Step 4: Handling Number Button Clicks

1. Implement functionality for number Buttons to append digits to the current expression:

```kotlin
```

```kotlin
private fun appendNumber(number: Int) {

    currentExpression += number

    updateResultView()

}
```

Step 5: Handling Operator Button Clicks

1. Implement functionality for operator Buttons to append operators to the current expression:

```kotlin
private fun appendOperator(operator: Char) {

    currentExpression += " $operator "

    updateResultView()

}
```

Step 6: Evaluating the Expression

1. Create a function to evaluate the current expression and update the result:

```kotlin
private fun evaluateExpression() {

    try {
```

```
        currentResult                                    =
ExpressionBuilder(currentExpression).build().evaluate()

        updateResultView()

    } catch (e: Exception) {

      currentResult = 0.0

      updateResultView()

    }

  }
```
```

Step 7: Updating the Result View

1. Implement a function to update the TextView displaying the current result:

```kotlin
  private fun updateResultView() {

    val                    resultTextView                =
findViewById<TextView>(R.id.resultTextView)

      resultTextView.text = currentExpression

  }
```
```

Step 8: Implementing Clear Functionality

1. Add functionality to clear the current expression and result:

```kotlin
private fun clear() {
    currentExpression = ""
    currentResult = 0.0
    updateResultView()
}
```

Step 9: Testing Your App

1. Run your app on an emulator or physical device.

2. Input numbers and operators using the Buttons.

3. Verify that the current expression and result update accordingly.

4. Test different arithmetic operations to ensure correct calculation.

Chapter 4:
Introducing Functions: Reusable Code Blocks

4.1: Defining Your First Function

As your programs grow more complex, writing and managing large numbers of code can become challenging and extremely difficult. This is where functions come in and make everything easier.

Functions are reusable blocks of code that perform specific tasks. They help you:

- ❖ Organize your code: Break down complex logic into smaller, manageable units.
- ❖ Improve code readability: Make your code easier to understand for yourself and others.
- ❖ Promote code reusability: Use the same functionality in different parts of your program without duplicating code.

You will be introduced to the fundamentals of defining and using functions in Kotlin.

Function definition: The process of creating a named block of code that performs a specific task.

Parameters: Optional values that you can pass to a function when you call it. These values are used within the function to perform its operations.

Return value: The value (if any) that a function can optionally return after its execution.

Imagine you are writing the same block of code repeatedly throughout your program. This can be tedious and error-prone. Thankfully, Kotlin offers a powerful solution: called functions.

Functions are reusable blocks of code that perform specific tasks. They help you organize your code, improve readability, and avoid redundancy.

4.1.1: The Basic Structure:

A function definition consists of several key elements:

Function name: A meaningful name that describes the function's purpose (e.g., `calculateArea`, `greetUser`).

Parameters (optional): Variables that accept values when the function is called. These values are used within the function's code block. Parameters are enclosed in parentheses following the function name.

Return type (optional): The data type of the value the function returns (e.g., `Int`, `String`, `Boolean`). If no value is explicitly returned, the function returns `Unit` by default, which signifies no meaningful return value.

Function body: The code block enclosed in curly braces `{}` that defines the actions the function performs.

Here's the basic structure of a function definition:

```kotlin
fun functionName(parameter1: dataType1, parameter2: dataType2, ...): returnType {
    // Code block containing the function's logic
```

```
}
```
```

### 4.1.2: Understanding Parameters and Return Values:

Parameters: Think of parameters as inputs to your function. You can define multiple parameters separated by commas within the parentheses. When you call the function, you provide actual values (arguments) that are assigned to these parameters within the function's body.

Return Values: A function can optionally return a value using the `return` keyword. This value becomes the output of the function and can be assigned to a variable or used in an expression when the function is called.

Example:

```kotlin
fun greetUser(name: String): String {

    val greeting = "Hello, $name!"

    return greeting // Function returns a String value (the greeting message)

}

val message = greetUser("Alice") // Function is called with argument "Alice"

println(message) // Output: Hello, Alice!
```

Benefits of Functions:

85
```

Reusability: Functions allow you to write a piece of code once and use it multiple times throughout your program. This saves time and effort.

Readability: By breaking down complex tasks into smaller functions, your code becomes easier to understand and maintain.

Modularity: Functions promote modularity, allowing you to focus on specific functionalities within each function.

4.2: Function Calls and Passing Arguments

Assuming you have a recipe for making your favorite cookies. In programming, functions work similarly. They are reusable blocks of code that perform specific tasks, just like following a recipe.

4.2.1: Calling Functions and Using Arguments:
A function definition specifies the steps involved in the task.

When you call a function, you're essentially telling the program to execute those steps.

Functions often require arguments, which are like the ingredients in your cookie recipe. These arguments provide the specific values the function needs to work with.

Example:

```kotlin
fun greet(name: String) { // Function definition with a name argument
```

```kotlin
    println("Hello, $name!")
}


val myName = "Alice"

greet(name = myName) // Calling the greet function with an argument
(myName)
```

From the above example

 We define a function called `greet` that takes a single argument named `name` of type `String`.

 Inside the function, we use a string template to personalize the greeting with the provided name.

 We then call the `greet` function, passing the value of the `myName` variable as the argument for the `name` parameter.

4.2.2: Return Values:
 Not all functions need to return a value. Some may simply perform actions like printing messages or modifying data.

 However, functions can also be designed to return a value after completing their task. This returned value can be used for further calculations or stored in a variable.

Example:

```kotlin
```

```
fun calculateArea(length: Double, width: Double): Double {  //
Function returning area

    return length  width

}
```

val rectangleArea = calculateArea(5.0, 3.0) // Calling the function, storing the returned value

println("The area of the rectangle is: $rectangleArea")

```
```

We define a function called `calculateArea` that takes two arguments, `length` and `width`, both of type `Double`.

Inside the function, we calculate the area and use the `return` keyword to send the result back.

When we call the function with specific values for `length` and `width`, the calculated area is stored in the `rectangleArea` variable.

4.2.3: Different Function Types:
We've seen functions with arguments and return values. There are other variations:

Functions without arguments: These functions can be used when a specific task needs to be performed without requiring any input values.

Functions with multiple arguments: Functions can handle multiple arguments, allowing you to pass in different pieces of data for processing.

By understanding and using functions effectively, you can break down complex tasks into smaller, reusable steps. This promotes cleaner, more modular code and makes your Android apps easier to maintain and understand.

4.3: Project 4: Building a Currency Converter App

Functionality:

The app will display a list of available currencies for both the source and target currency.

The user will enter the amount they want to convert.

The app will calculate the converted amount based on the selected currencies and current exchange rates.

The app will display the converted amount along with the currencies involved.

Steps:

1. Setting Up the Data:

Define a data structure (like a map or list) to store the supported currencies and their exchange rates. You can either:

Use hardcoded exchange rates within your code (for simplicity in this project).

Implement functionality to fetch live exchange rates from an API (more advanced approach).

```kotlin
val exchangeRates = mapOf(

    "USD" to 1.0, // US Dollar (base currency)

    "EUR" to 0.92, // Euro

    "GBP" to 0.82, // British Pound

    "JPY" to 114.16 // Japanese Yen

)
```

2. User Input and Currency Selection:

Display a user-friendly interface with:

A list or dropdown menu for selecting the source and target currencies.

A text field for entering the amount to convert.

A button to initiate the conversion.

Capture user input for the source currency, target currency, and amount to convert.

3. Implementing the Conversion Logic:

Define a function that performs the currency conversion calculation:

```kotlin
```

```
fun convertCurrency(amount: Double, fromCurrency: String,
toCurrency: String): Double {

    val exchangeRate = exchangeRates[toCurrency] ?: 0.0 // Handle
unsupported currencies

    return amount  exchangeRate

}
```

This function takes three arguments:

`amount`: The amount to be converted (entered by the user).

`fromCurrency`: The source currency selected by the user.

`toCurrency`: The target currency selected by the user.

It retrieves the exchange rate for the target currency from the `exchangeRates` map (or sets it to 0.0 if the currency is not supported).

Finally, it multiplies the amount by the exchange rate to calculate the converted amount.

4. Displaying the Result:

Once the conversion is calculated, display the converted amount to the user in a clear and formatted way.

You can use string formatting or dedicated libraries for currency formatting.

```kotlin
val convertedAmount = convertCurrency(amount, fromCurrency, toCurrency)

println("$amount $fromCurrency is equivalent to $convertedAmount $toCurrency")
```

5. Putting it all Together:

Combine the user interface elements, input handling, conversion logic, and result display into a cohesive application flow.

This is a simplified example for learning purposes.

In a real Android app, you'll utilize appropriate UI components like TextViews, Spinners, EditTexts, and Buttons to create a user-friendly interface.

You can enhance the app by:

Fetching live exchange rates from an online API.

Adding features like historical exchange rate charts or the ability to specify the conversion date.

Implementing error handling for invalid user input or unsupported currencies.

Alternative 2

Step 1: Setting Up Your Project

1. Open Android Studio and create a new project.

2. Choose a project name and select "Empty Activity" as the template.

3. Follow the prompts to set up your project, including choosing a package name and selecting your target API level.

Step 2: Designing the User Interface

1. Open the `activity_main.xml` layout file.

2. Design the layout to include EditText fields for entering the amount and Spinner dropdowns for selecting the currencies.

3. Add a Button to trigger the currency conversion.

Step 3: Writing Kotlin Code

1. Open the `MainActivity.kt` file.

2. Define a function to handle the currency conversion calculation:

```kotlin
fun convertCurrency(amount: Double, fromCurrency: String, toCurrency: String): Double {
    // Perform currency conversion logic here
    // Use exchange rates or an API to fetch real-time exchange rates
    // For simplicity, we'll use a hardcoded conversion rate
```

```kotlin
    val conversionRate = 1.23 // Example conversion rate from USD to
EUR

    return amount  conversionRate

}
```

3. Implement a function to retrieve the user's input and trigger the currency conversion:

```kotlin
fun convertButtonClicked() {
    val amountEditText =
findViewById<EditText>(R.id.amountEditText)
    val fromCurrencySpinner =
findViewById<Spinner>(R.id.fromCurrencySpinner)
    val toCurrencySpinner =
findViewById<Spinner>(R.id.toCurrencySpinner)

    val amount = amountEditText.text.toString().toDouble()

    val fromCurrency = fromCurrencySpinner.selectedItem.toString()

    val toCurrency = toCurrencySpinner.selectedItem.toString()
```

```kotlin
    val convertedAmount = convertCurrency(amount, fromCurrency,
toCurrency)


    // Display the converted amount to the user

    val                        resultTextView                        =
findViewById<TextView>(R.id.resultTextView)

    resultTextView.text = "Converted Amount: $convertedAmount
$toCurrency"

}
```

Step 4: Setting Up UI Event Handling

1. Bind the `convertButtonClicked` function to the Button's
   onClick event in the `onCreate` method:

```kotlin
override fun onCreate(savedInstanceState: Bundle?) {

    super.onCreate(savedInstanceState)

    setContentView(R.layout.activity_main)


    val convertButton = findViewById<Button>(R.id.convertButton)

    convertButton.setOnClickListener {

        convertButtonClicked()
```

```
    }
}
```
```


Step 5: Testing Your App

1. Run your app on an emulator or physical device.

2. Enter an amount in the EditText field, select the currencies to convert from and to, and click the "Convert" button.

3. Observe the converted amount displayed on the screen.
```

Chapter 5:
Data Structures: Organizing Your Data

5.1: Exploring Lists: Collections of Ordered Items

We all have a shopping list or a to-do list. These are essentially collections of items that we want to keep track of in a specific order. In Kotlin, lists provide a similar functionality for storing and managing collections of elements in an ordered manner.

Understanding Lists:

A list is a collection of items that can hold elements of the same data type or even different data types (depending on how the list is defined).

Elements within a list are ordered, meaning each item has a specific position or index.

The first element has an index of 0, the second element has an index of 1, and so on.

Creating Lists:

There are two main ways to create lists in Kotlin:

1. Using the `listOf` function:

This is a convenient way to create immutable (read-only) lists. Once created, you cannot modify the elements within the list.

```kotlin
```

```kotlin
val fruitsList = listOf("apple", "banana", "cherry")
```

2. Using the `mutableListOf` function:

This function creates mutable lists, which means you can add, remove, or change elements after the list is created.

```kotlin
val shoppingList = mutableListOf("bread", "milk", "eggs")
```

Accessing Elements:

You can access elements in a list using their index within square brackets `[]`.

```kotlin
val firstFruit = fruitsList[0] // firstFruit will be "apple"
```

Kotlin list indexing starts from 0, so the last element will have an index equal to the list size minus 1. It's important to avoid accessing elements with out-of-range indexes as this can lead to errors.

Iterating over Lists:

Using for loop: This is a common way to process each element in a list one by one. The loop variable iterates through the indices of the list.

```kotlin
for (fruit in fruitsList) {

    println(fruit) // Prints each fruit on a new line

}
```

Using forEach loop (with lambda expressions):

This is a more concise way to iterate over a list and perform an action on each element.

```kotlin
fruitsList.forEach { fruit -> println(fruit) }
```

Lists are fundamental building blocks for working with collections of data in Kotlin programs. By understanding how to create, access, and iterate through lists, you'll be well-equipped to tackle various tasks in your Android app development journey.

5.2: Working with Maps: Key-Value Pairs

You have a phonebook where you store names (keys) and corresponding phone numbers (values). In programming, maps provide a similar functionality. They are a fundamental data structure used to store collections of key-value pairs.

Key: A unique identifier used to access a specific value within the map. Keys can be of various data types like strings, integers, or even custom objects.

Value: The data associated with a particular key. Values can also be of various data types.

Maps are efficient for situations where you need to quickly access data based on a unique identifier (the key). Here's why they're useful:

Organized Data Storage: Maps keep your data organized by associating each value with a specific key, making retrieval and management efficient.

Fast Lookup: Since keys are unique, accessing a value in a map is very fast, similar to how you can quickly find a phone number in a phonebook by looking up the name (key).

Common Operations with Maps:

Adding Elements (Putting): Use the `put` function to add a new key-value pair to the map.

```kotlin
val phonebook = mutableMapOf<String, String>() // Creates a mutable map

phonebook.put("Alice", "123-456-7890")
```

Accessing Elements (Getting): Use the `get` function to retrieve the value associated with a specific key.

```kotlin
val aliceNumber = phonebook.get("Alice") // aliceNumber will be "123-456-7890"
```

Checking for Existence (Contains): Use the `containsKey` function to check if a specific key exists in the map.

```kotlin
val hasBobsNumber = phonebook.containsKey("Bob") // hasBobsNumber will be false (assuming "Bob" is not added)
```

Removing Elements: Use the `remove` function to delete a key-value pair from the map.

```kotlin
phonebook.remove("Alice") // Removes the key-value pair for "Alice"
```

Things to Remember:

Keys in a map must be unique. You cannot have two key-value pairs with the same key.

The order in which elements are added to the map is generally not preserved when iterating through it.

5.3: Project 5: Building a Contact List App

Functionality:

❖ Users can add new contacts with details like name, phone number, and email address.
❖ The app will store the contact information in a structured format for easy access.
❖ Users can view the list of all saved contacts.
❖ Users can search for specific contacts by name. (Optional: You can expand this to search by other criteria later)

Steps:

1. Defining a Contact Model:

Create a data structure (like a class) to represent a single contact. This "Contact" class will hold the properties for each contact's information.

```kotlin
data class Contact(val name: String, val phoneNumber: String, val email: String)
```

This `Contact` class defines three properties:

`name`: The name of the contact (String).

`phoneNumber`: The phone number of the contact (String).

`email`: The email address of the contact (String).

2. Using Lists and Maps for Storage:

There are two primary approaches to store contact information:

List: A simple list of `Contact` objects can be used for smaller datasets. Adding and removing contacts is straightforward with list operations.

```kotlin
val contacts = mutableListOf<Contact>()
```

Map: A map is more efficient for larger datasets, especially when searching for contacts by name. The map key can be the contact's name, and the value can be the corresponding `Contact` object.

```kotlin
val contacts = mutableMapOf<String, Contact>()
```

3. Implementing Add Contact Functionality:

 Define a function to handle adding new contacts.

 Prompt the user for the contact's name, phone number, and email.

 Create a new `Contact` object with the entered information.

 Add the new `Contact` object to the chosen data structure (list or map).

4. Displaying the Contact List:

 Define a function to iterate through the contacts list or map and display each contact's information in a user-friendly format.

5. Searching for Contacts (Optional):

If using a list, you can iterate through the list and compare names with the search term.

If using a map, you can directly access the contact information using the name as the key.

Display the search results or indicate if no matching contact is found.

Here's an example code snippet demonstrating basic functionalities (using a list):

```kotlin
fun addContact() {
    print("Enter name: ")
    val name = readLine() ?: ""
    print("Enter phone number: ")
    val phoneNumber = readLine() ?: ""
    print("Enter email: ")
    val email = readLine() ?: ""

    val newContact = Contact(name, phoneNumber, email)
    contacts.add(newContact)
    println("Contact added successfully!")
```

```kotlin
}

fun displayContacts() {
    if (contacts.isEmpty()) {
        println("There are no contacts in the list.")
        return
    }

    println("Contacts:")
    for (contact in contacts) {
        println("Name: ${contact.name}")
        println("Phone Number: ${contact.phoneNumber}")
        println("Email: ${contact.email}")
        println("-------")
    }
}

fun main() {
    while (true) {
        println("Menu:")
```

```
        println("1. Add Contact")

        println("2. View Contacts")

        println("3. Exit")


        val choice = readLine()?.toIntOrNull() ?: 0


        when (choice) {

            1 -> addContact()

            2 -> displayContacts()

            3 -> break

            else -> println("Invalid choice.")

        }

    }

}
```

Android app, you'll utilize UI components for user interaction and data display.

You can enhance the app by:

Implementing functionalities like editing or deleting contacts.

Sorting the contact list by different criteria (name, phone number, etc.).

Choose the appropriate data structure (list or map) based on your anticipated app usage and the size of your expected contact list.

Chapter 6:
Getting User Input: Interacting with the User

6.1: Understanding User Input Methods

In any interactive application, collecting user input is crucial for gathering information and responding to user actions. Android offers various ways to capture user input through different UI elements.

Common User Input Methods:

➢ Text Fields (EditText):

A versatile component for entering text input.

You can define the type of text allowed (e.g., plain text, email address, numbers) using the `android:inputType` attribute in your XML layout file.

In your code, access the user-entered text using the `getText().toString()` method on the EditText object.

➢ Buttons (Button):

Buttons are used to trigger actions when clicked.

You can set the button text to indicate the action it performs.

In your code, listen for click events on the button using an `OnClickListener`. When the button is clicked, the `onClick` method of the listener will be called, allowing you to execute code based on the user's action.

➢ Checkboxes (CheckBox):

Allow users to select one or more options from a set of choices.

Each checkbox represents a boolean value (true or false).

In your code, access the checked state of a checkbox using the `isChecked()` method and respond accordingly.

➢ Radio Buttons (RadioButton):

Similar to checkboxes, but only one radio button can be selected at a time within a group.

Useful for presenting mutually exclusive options.

Access the checked state of a radio button using the `isChecked()` method and determine which option the user selected.

➢ Spinners (Spinner):

Provide a dropdown menu for users to select an item from a predefined list.

Useful for presenting a limited set of options in a compact way.

In your code, access the selected item from the spinner using the `getSelectedItem()` method.

Handling Different Input Types:

 As mentioned earlier, you can specify the expected input type for text fields using `android:inputType` in your layout file. Here are some common options:

`text`: Plain text (default)

`number`: Numeric input

`textPassword`: Password input (characters hidden)

`textEmailAddress`: Email address input

You can also perform additional validation in your code to ensure the user enters the data in the expected format. For example, you might check if a number field contains only digits before processing it further.

Choosing the appropriate user input method depends on the type of data you want to collect and how you want to present it to the user.

Consider user experience (UX) when designing your app's interface. Make it clear and intuitive for users to understand how to provide input.

6.2: Validating User Input: Ensuring Accuracy

In any interactive program, user input plays a crucial role. However, it's essential to make sure the user provides valid information to avoid errors and maintain a smooth user experience. This is where input validation comes in.

What is Input Validation?

Input validation is the process of checking user input to ensure it meets specific criteria before accepting it. This helps prevent errors that might occur due to invalid data being used in your program.

Benefits of Input Validation:

❖ Prevents program crashes: By catching invalid input early on, you can avoid unexpected behavior or crashes that could frustrate users.

❖ Improves data integrity: Ensures the data your program works with is accurate and reliable.

❖ Enhances user experience: Provides clear feedback to users when they enter incorrect information, helping them correct their input and avoid frustration.

Common Input Validation Techniques:

Here are some common techniques you can use for input validation in Kotlin:

Data Type Checks:

Make sure the entered data matches the expected data type (e.g., checking if a string can be converted to a number).

Range Checks:

Limit user input to a specific range of values (e.g., ensuring an age is within a valid range).

Non-Empty Checks:

Prevent users from leaving required fields blank.

Pattern Matching:

Use regular expressions to verify if the input follows a specific format (e.g., email address format).

Implementing Input Validation in the Currency Converter App (Project 4):

Let's revisit Project 4 (Currency Converter) and add input validation:

Non-Empty Checks:

Ensure the user enters a value in the amount field before attempting the conversion.

Display a message like "Please enter an amount to convert." if the field is empty.

Data Type Checks:

Since the amount needs to be a number, try converting the user-entered value to a Double using `toDoubleOrNull()`.

If the conversion fails (returns null), display a message like "Please enter a valid number for the amount."

Example Code (using improvements to Project 4):

```kotlin
fun convertCurrency(amount: Double, fromCurrency: String, toCurrency: String): Double {
    // ... (conversion logic remains the same)
}


var amountStr = readLine()
if (amountStr.isEmpty()) {
    println("Please enter an amount to convert.")
    return
}


val amount = amountStr.toDoubleOrNull() ?: 0.0 // Handle non-numeric input
```

```
if (amount == 0.0) {

    println("Please enter a valid number for the amount.")

    return

}


// ... proceed with conversion logic using the validated amount
```
```

There are various ways to implement input validation depending on your specific needs.

Always provide clear and informative feedback messages to users when they enter invalid data.

By implementing proper input validation, you can significantly improve the robustness and user experience of your Android apps.


## 6.3: Project 6: Building a To-Do List App

Functionality:

Users can add new tasks to the list by providing a description.

Each task will be displayed with its description and a checkbox for marking completion.

Users can edit existing tasks by modifying their descriptions.
```

Users can mark tasks as completed by checking the corresponding checkbox.

Steps:

1. Data Model:

Define a data structure to represent a single task item. This can be a simple class:

```kotlin
data class Task(val description: String, var isCompleted: Boolean)
```

The `Task` class has two properties:

  `description`: A string representing the task description.

  `isCompleted`: A boolean flag indicating whether the task is completed (true) or not (false).

2. Task List:

Create a mutable list to store all the tasks in your to-do list app. You can use an `ArrayList` or a more advanced collection type like `MutableList<Task>`.

```kotlin
val tasks = mutableListOf<Task>()
```

3. User Interface (Optional):

In a real Android app, you'll utilize UI components like:

An EditText for users to enter the task description.

A Button to add the new task.

A ListView or RecyclerView to display the list of tasks.

Checkboxes associated with each task for marking completion.

EditTexts or additional buttons for editing existing tasks.

For simplicity, this example will focus on the logic behind the functionalities.

4. Adding Tasks:

Define a function to add a new task to the list:

```kotlin
fun addTask(description: String) {
    val newTask = Task(description, false) // Create a new Task object
    tasks.add(newTask) // Add the new task to the list
}
```

This function takes the user-provided `description` as input.

It creates a new `Task` object with the given description and sets `isCompleted` to false (not completed initially).

Finally, it adds the new task object to the `tasks` list.

5. Editing Tasks:

Implement functionality to locate the specific task to be edited based on user input (e.g., task index or unique identifier).

Allow users to modify the `description` property of the corresponding `Task` object in the list.

6. Marking Tasks as Complete:

Define a function to handle marking tasks complete:

```kotlin
fun markTaskComplete(index: Int) {
    if (index >= 0 && index < tasks.size) {
        tasks[index].isCompleted = true // Toggle the isCompleted flag
    } else {
        println("Invalid task index!") // Handle invalid input (optional)
    }
```

```
}
```
```
```

This function takes the index of the task in the `tasks` list as input.

It checks if the provided index is within the valid range of the list.

If the index is valid, it accesses the corresponding `Task` object and sets its `isCompleted` flag to true, marking it as complete.

7. Displaying the To-Do List (Optional):

In a real app, iterate through the `tasks` list and display each task's description along with its corresponding checkbox state (checked for completed tasks).

This is a simplified example for learning purposes.

In Android app would involve building a user interface with appropriate components and handling user interaction effectively.

You can enhance the app by:

Persisting tasks to storage (e.g., SharedPreferences or Room database) to save the list even after the app is closed.

Implementing features like task prioritization, due dates, and categorizing tasks.

Adding functionality to delete tasks from the list.

Chapter 7:
Working with Layouts: Building User Interfaces

7.1: Exploring the Basics of Android Layouts

The user interface (UI) is what your users see and interact with in your Android app. It's the visual layer that allows users to navigate, input information, and view results. Building a user-friendly and visually appealing UI is crucial for creating a successful app.

The Building Blocks of Your UI:

Views: The fundamental building blocks of your UI are views. These represent individual UI elements like buttons, text fields, images, and more. Each view has its own properties and behaviors.

Layouts: Layouts are like containers that organize and arrange views on the screen. They define the structure and hierarchy of your UI, determining how views are positioned and interact with each other.

Resources: Resources are additional elements used to customize the appearance and behavior of your app. This can include things like images, colors, fonts, and even string values displayed to the user.

Think of Layouts as Blueprints:

Imagine a blueprint for a house. The blueprint defines the arrangement of rooms, doors, windows, and other elements. Similarly, layouts in your app act as blueprints for your UI. They specify how each view (like a button or text field) is positioned on the screen and how they interact with each other.

Common Layout Types:

Android provides various layout types to suit different UI needs. Here are a few popular ones:

LinearLayout: Arranges views in a single row (horizontal) or column (vertical).

FrameLayout: Positions views on top of each other, with the last view added typically being on top.

RelativeLayout: Offers more flexibility by allowing you to position views relative to each other or the parent layout.

ConstraintLayout: A powerful layout type offering precise control over view positioning using constraints.

Project Idea: "Simple Profile Screen":

In this project, we'll build a basic profile screen layout using an XML file. We'll use either LinearLayout or FrameLayout to arrange the UI elements:

Avatar Image: A small image representing the user's profile picture.

Username: Text displaying the user's name.

Bio Text: A short description about the user.

Choosing a Layout:

We can achieve this layout using either LinearLayout or FrameLayout:

 LinearLayout: Arranges elements horizontally (by default) or vertically (with `android:orientation="vertical"`).

 FrameLayout: Stacks elements on top of each other, with the last element on top.

Steps:

1. Create a New Android Project:

  - Open Android Studio and start a new project. Choose "Empty Activity" as the template and give it a name like "SimpleProfileScreen".

2. Create the Layout File (XML):

  - Right-click on the `res` folder in the project directory and select "New -> Android resource file".

  - Choose "Layout resource file" and name it "activity_main.xml" (following naming conventions).

3. Design the Layout using LinearLayout:

  - Open the `activity_main.xml` file and paste the following code:

```xml
<?xml version="1.0" encoding="utf-8"?>
<LinearLayout
xmlns:android="http://schemas.android.com/apk/res/android"
    android:layout_width="match_parent"
    android:layout_height="match_parent"
    android:orientation="vertical"
    android:padding="16dp">  <ImageView
        android:id="@+id/avatar_image"
        android:layout_width="100dp"
        android:layout_height="100dp"
        android:src="@drawable/ic_avatar"
android:layout_gravity="center_horizontal"
android:layout_marginBottom="16dp" />  <TextView
        android:id="@+id/username_text"
        android:layout_width="wrap_content"
        android:layout_height="wrap_content"
        android:text="John Doe"
        android:textSize="20sp"
        android:textStyle="bold"
        android:layout_gravity="center_horizontal" />  <TextView
```

```
    android:id="@+id/bio_text"

    android:layout_width="wrap_content"

    android:layout_height="wrap_content"

    android:text="Software Developer"

    android:textSize="16sp" />


</LinearLayout>
```

The `LinearLayout` is the root element, defining a vertical layout for all child elements.

`android:padding` adds padding around the entire layout for better spacing.

Each child element (ImageView and TextViews) has its properties defined:

`android:id`: Unique identifier for referencing the element in code.

`android:layout_width` and `android:layout_height`: Define the element's size or behavior (e.g., `wrap_content` for automatic sizing).

`android:src`: For the ImageView, specifies the image resource (replace with your image).

`android:text`: For TextViews, sets the displayed text.

`android:textSize` and `android:textStyle`: Customize text size and style.

`android:layout_gravity="center_horizontal"` (optional): Centers the image and username text horizontally within their available space.

`android:layout_marginBottom` (optional): Adds margin below the image for spacing.

4. Design the Layout using FrameLayout:

- You can achieve a similar layout using FrameLayout. Here's the modified code:

```xml
<FrameLayout xmlns:android="http://schemas.android.com/apk/res/android"
    android:layout_width="match_parent"
    android:layout_height="match_parent"
    android:padding="16dp">

    <ImageView
        android:id="@+id/avatar_image"
        android:layout_width="100dp"
        android:layout_height="100dp"
        android:src="@drawable/ic_avatar"
        android:layout_gravity="center" />
```

7.2: Building Layouts with XML:

In Android app development, layouts are the fundamental building blocks for creating user interfaces (UIs). They define the arrangement and organization of UI elements like buttons, text views, images, and more. But how do we tell Android how to structure these elements on the screen? This is where XML comes in.

XML (Extensible Markup Language) is a simple, human-readable language used to define the structure and attributes of your app's layouts. It's like a blueprint that tells Android how to arrange the UI elements on the screen.

Understanding the Structure:

An XML layout file typically consists of the following elements:

Root Element: Every layout file has a root element that defines the overall layout type. Common layout types include LinearLayout, FrameLayout, RelativeLayout, and ConstraintLayout (we'll explore these in more detail later).

Child Elements: Nested within the root element are child elements that represent individual UI components like TextView, Button, ImageView, etc. Each child element has attributes that specify its properties and configuration.

Attributes for Configuration:

Each UI element (child element) within the layout has attributes that define its characteristics. Here are some common attributes you'll encounter:

`android:layout_width`: Defines the width of the element (e.g., `match_parent` to span the entire width or `wrap_content` to fit the content).

`android:layout_height`: Defines the height of the element (similar options as `layout_width`).

`android:text`: Sets the text content for elements like TextView.

`android:id`: Assigns a unique identifier to an element for referencing it later in your code.

Many more! There are numerous attributes depending on the specific UI element type.

Nesting Layouts for Complex UIs:

Layouts can be nested within each other to create hierarchical structures for complex UIs. Imagine a news article screen with a headline, an image, and body text. You could use a parent layout (e.g., LinearLayout) to arrange two child layouts:

One child layout for the headline and image (using another layout type like FrameLayout to position them side-by-side).

Another child layout for the body text (e.g., a ScrollView to allow scrollable content).

By nesting layouts, you can achieve intricate UI structures and organize your app's screens effectively.

Assessment

Project Idea: "News Article Screen": Design a news article screen layout using nested layouts to arrange elements like a headline, image, and body text with proper spacing and alignment.

7.3: Enhancing Layouts with Properties and Attributes:

7.3.1: Layout Properties - Controlling Positioning and Behavior

Layout properties are essential for defining the size, position, and behavior of UI elements within your layouts. Here are some key properties to understand:

`android:layout_width` and `android:layout_height`: These properties determine the width and height of an element, respectively. You can specify them in various units like `dp` (density-independent pixels), `match_parent` (match the size of the parent layout), or `wrap_content` (adjust the size to fit the element's content).

`android:layout_gravity`: This property controls how an element is positioned within its parent layout. Common values include `center`, `top`, `bottom`, `left`, and `right`, allowing you to align elements horizontally or vertically.

`android:layout_margin` and `android:layout_padding`: These properties define the spacing around an element. `margin` specifies the outer space between the element and its borders, while `padding` defines the space between the element's content and its borders. Both can be set in various units for precise control.

7.3.2: Attributes for Style and Appearance

Attributes go beyond layout and allow you to customize the visual appearance of your UI elements. Here are some commonly used attributes:

`android:background`: This attribute sets the background color or image for an element. You can use color resource identifiers or image resource references to define the background.

`android:textColor`: This attribute determines the text color of an element like a TextView or Button. You can specify colors using color resource identifiers or hex codes.

`android:textSize`: This attribute controls the font size of text elements. You can specify the size in various units like `sp` (scaled pixels).

`android:textStyle`: This attribute allows you to set the style of the text, such as `bold` or `italic`.

By effectively combining layout properties and attributes, you can achieve precise control over the structure, positioning, and visual style of your UI elements, resulting in a well-organized and visually appealing user interface for your Android app.

7.3.3: Applying Properties and Attributes in Practice

Here's an example to illustrate how properties and attributes work together:

Imagine designing a login screen layout with an email address text field and a login button. Here's a snippet of how the layout might look in XML:

```xml
<LinearLayout
    android:layout_width="match_parent"
    android:layout_height="match_parent"
    android:orientation="vertical"
    android:gravity="center">

    <EditText
        android:id="@+id/email_field"
        android:layout_width="match_parent"
        android:layout_height="wrap_content"
        android:hint="Enter your email address"
        android:inputType="textEmailAddress"
        android:padding="16dp"
        android:background="@drawable/rounded_border"
```

```
        android:textColor="@color/primary_text_color" />


    <Button
        android:id="@+id/login_button"
        android:layout_width="wrap_content"
        android:layout_height="wrap_content"
        android:text="Login"
        android:background="@color/accent_color"
        android:textColor="@android:color/white"
        android:layout_marginTop="16dp" />


</LinearLayout>
```

The `LinearLayout` is the parent layout with `match_parent` width and height, filling the entire screen.

The `EditText` for the email field has:

    `match_parent` width, stretching across the screen.

    `wrap_content` height, adjusting to the content size.

    `android:hint` for placeholder text.

    `android:inputType` set to `textEmailAddress` for email input.

    `android:padding` of 16dp for spacing around the text.

A custom drawable `@drawable/rounded_border` set as the background.

Text color set to `@color/primary_text_color` from your app's color resources.

 The `Button` for login has:

`wrap_content` for both width and height, menyesuaikan ukuran [menyesuaikan ukuran = adjusting the size] to fit the button text.

Text set to "Login".

Background color set to `@color/accent_color` from your app's color resources.

Text color set to white using the system color constant `@android:color/white`.

`android:layout_marginTop` of 16dp to add space above the button.

Project Idea: "Custom Contact List Item":

In this project, you'll design a custom layout for a single contact item within a contact list application. This layout will utilize properties and attributes to arrange, size, and style the elements effectively.

Here's what you'll build:

A visually appealing and informative contact list item layout featuring:

Avatar Image: A circular image representing the contact's profile picture.

Contact Name: The contact's name displayed in a bold font.

Phone Number: The contact's phone number displayed below the name in a smaller font.

Here's how you can achieve this using a custom layout:

1. Create a New Layout Resource File:

   - In your Android Studio project, right-click on the `layout` folder within your resource directory and select "New -> Layout resource file".

   - Name the file `contact_item.xml`.

2. Design the Layout Structure:

   - Within the `contact_item.xml` file, use a `LinearLayout` as the root element to arrange the contact information horizontally.

3. Add the Avatar Image:

   - Inside the `LinearLayout`, include an `ImageView` element.

   - Set the `android:layout_width` and `android:layout_height` to a fixed size in `dp` (e.g., 50dp) to create a square image.

- Use the `android:src` attribute to specify the placeholder image resource (or dynamically set it based on the actual contact data).

- Set the `android:layout_gravity` to `centerVertical` to align the image vertically within the layout.

4. Design the Contact Information Area:

- Inside the `LinearLayout`, add another `LinearLayout` oriented vertically to stack the contact name and phone number.

5. Add the Contact Name:

- Inside the nested `LinearLayout`, include a `TextView` element.

- Set the text content using the `android:text` attribute (or dynamically set it based on the contact data).

- Use `android:textStyle` set to `bold` to make the name stand out.

- Set a slightly larger text size using `android:textSize` in `sp`.

6. Add the Phone Number:

- Below the name, add another `TextView` element within the nested `LinearLayout`.

- Set the text content using `android:text` (or dynamically set it based on the contact data).

- Use a slightly smaller text size compared to the name using `android:textSize` in `sp`.

7. Styling and Spacing:

- Use `android:padding` on both the root `LinearLayout` and the nested `LinearLayout` to create some space between the elements and the layout edges.

- Consider setting a background color for the contact item layout using `android:background` for better visual separation.

You can customize the layout further by adding a divider line between contact items or using a custom font for the contact name.

Alternative 2

Project Idea: Custom Contact List Item (Code Example)

Here's the code for the custom layout file (`contact_item.xml`):

```xml
<?xml version="1.0" encoding="utf-8"?>
<LinearLayout
xmlns:android="http://schemas.android.com/apk/res/android"
    android:layout_width="match_parent"
    android:layout_height="wrap_content"
    android:orientation="horizontal"
    android:padding="8dp">  <ImageView
        android:id="@+id/contact_avatar"
        android:layout_width="50dp"
        android:layout_height="50dp"
        android:layout_gravity="centerVertical"
        android:src="@drawable/ic_person_placeholder"  />

    <LinearLayout
        android:layout_width="0dp"
android:layout_height="wrap_content"
```

```xml
        android:layout_marginStart="8dp"
android:orientation="vertical">


    <TextView

        android:id="@+id/contact_name"

        android:layout_width="wrap_content"

        android:layout_height="wrap_content"

        android:text="John Doe"  android:textColor="@color/black"

        android:textSize="16sp"

        android:textStyle="bold" />


    <TextView

        android:id="@+id/contact_phone_number"

        android:layout_width="wrap_content"

        android:layout_height="wrap_content"

        android:text="123-456-7890"
android:textColor="@color/gray"

        android:textSize="14sp" />


    </LinearLayout>
```

</LinearLayout>

```
```

Explanation:

1. Root Layout (`LinearLayout`):

   - `android:layout_width="match_parent"`: Stretches the layout horizontally to fill the available space.

   - `android:layout_height="wrap_content"`: Allows the layout to adjust its height based on the content within.

   - `android:orientation="horizontal"`: Arranges child elements (avatar and information) side-by-side.

   - `android:padding="8dp"`: Adds some padding around the elements for better spacing.

2. Avatar Image (`ImageView`):

   - `android:id="@+id/contact_avatar"`: Assigns a unique identifier for referencing the view in code.

   - `android:layout_width` and `android:layout_height` set to 50dp for a square image.

   - `android:layout_gravity="centerVertical"`: Aligns the image vertically within the layout.

   - `android:src="@drawable/ic_person_placeholder"`: Sets a placeholder image resource (replace with dynamic data later).

3. Contact Information Container (`LinearLayout`):

  - `android:layout_width="0dp"`: Allows this layout to occupy the remaining space after the avatar.

  - `android:layout_height="wrap_content"`: Adjusts the height based on the content inside.

  - `android:layout_marginStart="8dp"`: Adds margin from the avatar image for separation.

  - `android:orientation="vertical"`: Stacks the name and phone number text views vertically.

4. Contact Name (`TextView`):

  - `android:id="@+id/contact_name"`: Unique identifier for referencing the text view in code.

  - `android:text="John Doe"`: Sets the contact name (replace with dynamic data).

  - `android:textColor="@color/black"`: Sets the text color to black (customize as needed).

  - `android:textSize="16sp"`: Sets the text size to 16sp.

  - `android:textStyle="bold"`: Makes the text bold for emphasis.

5. Phone Number (`TextView`):

  - Similar properties as the contact name text view, but with a smaller text size (14sp) and potentially a different color (gray).

This code provides a basic structure. You can customize it further by:

Adding a background color to

Chapter 8:
Working with Strings and Text Manipulation

8.1: Understanding Strings and Characters:

In the world of programming, we often deal with textual data. Kotlin provides a powerful tool called the String type to represent and manipulate this kind of information.

What is a String?
A String is a collection of characters that form text. It's like a sequence of letters, numbers, symbols, or even spaces that you can use to represent words, sentences, or any textual content.

Accessing Individual Characters:
Just like items in a list, characters within a String can be accessed one by one using their position (index). The index starts from 0, meaning the first character is at index 0, the second at index 1, and so on.

```kotlin
val greeting = "Hello, world!"

val firstLetter = greeting[0] // This will be 'H'
val lastLetter = greeting[greeting.length - 1] // This will be '!' (accessing the last character)
```

Important Note: You cannot modify individual characters within a String in Kotlin. If you need to change the content, you'll create a new String with the desired modifications.

Creating and Manipulating Strings:

Kotlin offers various ways to work with Strings:

String Literals: You can directly enclose text in double quotes ("") to create a String literal.

```kotlin
val name = "Alice"
```

String Concatenation: The plus operator (+) allows you to join (concatenate) multiple Strings into a single String.

```kotlin
val fullName = name + " Smith" // This will create "Alice Smith"
```

Template Literals: Template literals (introduced with backticks ``) provide a more flexible way to incorporate variables or expressions within a String.

```kotlin
val age = 25
```

val message = "Hello, my name is $name and I'm $age years old."
```

String Methods: Kotlin provides built-in methods for various String operations:

`length`: Returns the number of characters in the String.

`toUpperCase()`: Converts the String to uppercase.

`toLowerCase()`: Converts the String to lowercase.

`trim()`: Removes leading and trailing whitespace characters.

`substring(startIndex, endIndex)`: Extracts a portion of the String as a new String based on the specified start and end indices.

Many more methods are available for advanced String manipulation!

Strings are immutable in Kotlin, meaning you cannot change the content of an existing String after creation.

Mastering String manipulation techniques is fundamental for working with textual data in your Kotlin programs.

## 8.2: Searching and Comparison:

When it comes to programming, strings are sequences of characters that represent text data. Working with strings effectively is fundamental for many tasks in Android development. This section dives into searching and comparing strings using built-in methods and operators in Kotlin.
```

8.2.1: Searching Within Strings

`contains(substring)` method:

This method checks if a specific substring (sequence of characters) exists within a string. It returns `true` if the substring is found, and `false` otherwise.

```kotlin
val message = "Hello, world!"

val hasWorld = message.contains("world") // Returns true
```

`indexOf(substring)` method:

This method locates the starting index of the first occurrence of a substring within a string. It returns the index position (integer) if the substring is found, or -1 if not found.

```kotlin
val message = "Hello, world!"

val worldIndex = message.indexOf("world") // Returns 7
```

8.2.2: Comparing Strings

Equality (`==`):

The double equals sign (`==`) operator checks if two strings have the same content, character by character.

```kotlin
val name1 = "Alice"

val name2 = "Alice"

val areEqual = name1 == name2 // Returns true (same content)
```

Case Sensitivity:

String comparisons in Kotlin are case-sensitive. "Hello" and "hello" are considered different strings.

To perform a case-insensitive comparison, you can use the `toLowerCase()` or `toUpperCase()` methods to convert both strings to the same case before comparison.


```kotlin
val name1 = "Alice"

val name2 = "aLIce"

val areEqual = name1.toLowerCase() == name2.toLowerCase() // Returns true (ignoring case)
```

Comparison Operators (`<`, `>`, `<=`, `>=`):

These operators can be used to compare strings lexicographically (based on alphabetical order, character by character).

145

```kotlin
val word1 = "Apple"

val word2 = "Banana"

val isBefore = word1 < word2 // Returns true ("Apple" comes before
"Banana" alphabetically)

```

8.3: Formatting Text Output:

In this section, we'll explore techniques for formatting and manipulating text data in your Kotlin programs.

8.3.1: String Formatting Techniques
String Templates:

String templates provide a clean way to embed variables directly within strings. They are enclosed in backticks (`) and allow you to insert variable values without explicit concatenation.

```kotlin
val name = "Alice"

val age = 30

val greeting = "Hello, my name is $name and I am $age years old."
```

println(greeting) // Output: Hello, my name is Alice and I am 30 years old.

```
```

In this example, the variable values `${name}` and `${age}` are directly inserted into the string template, resulting in a formatted greeting message.

String Interpolation:

String interpolation is a simpler technique for inserting expressions within strings. You can use `${expression}` directly inside a string literal.

```kotlin
val message = "Welcome " + name + "! You are " + age + " years old."

println(message)  // Output: Welcome Alice! You are 30 years old.


// Using string interpolation for the same message:

val message = "Welcome ${name}! You are ${age} years old."

println(message)  // Output: Welcome Alice! You are 30 years old.
```

Both approaches achieve the same result. String templates are generally preferred for readability, especially when dealing with complex expressions within the string.

8.3.2: String Manipulation Methods

Kotlin provides various methods for manipulating strings:

`toUpperCase()` and `toLowerCase()`:

These methods convert a string to uppercase or lowercase, respectively.


```kotlin
val fullName = "JoHn dOe"

val allUppercase = fullName.toUpperCase()  // allUppercase will be "JOHN DOE"

val allLowercase = fullName.toLowerCase()  // allLowercase will be "john doe"
```


`trim()`:

This method removes leading and trailing whitespace characters (spaces, tabs, newlines) from a string.

```kotlin
val messyString = "  Extra spaces at the beginning and end  "

val trimmedString = messyString.trim()   // trimmedString will be "Extra spaces at the beginning and end"
```

`substring()`:

This method extracts a portion of a string based on starting and ending index positions.

```kotlin
val quote = "Never stop learning."

val firstWord = quote.substring(0, 5)  // firstWord will be "Never"
```

By mastering these techniques, you'll be able to format text output for display, convert strings to different cases, clean user input, and extract specific parts of strings as needed in your Kotlin programs.

8.4: Project 8: Building a Password Generator App:

In this project, we'll create a Password Generator App using Kotlin. The app will generate random passwords based on user-defined criteria, such as length and complexity requirements. We'll go through each step of the process, from designing the app to building the user interface and implementing the password generation logic.

Step 1: Designing the App

Before diving into coding, it's essential to define the type of passwords our app will generate. We'll consider factors such as the length of the password and any complexity requirements, such as including uppercase letters, lowercase letters, numbers, and special characters. For example, we might decide that our app will generate passwords with a minimum length of 8 characters, including at least one uppercase letter, one lowercase letter, one number, and one special character.

Step 2: Generating Random Characters

To generate random characters for our passwords, we'll utilize Kotlin's built-in random number generation capabilities. We'll create a function that generates a random character based on the specified criteria (e.g., uppercase, lowercase, number, special character). We'll then use this function to generate each character of the password according to the user's requirements.

Step 3: Building the User Interface

In this step, we'll design the user interface (UI) for our app. The UI will include elements for users to specify the length of the password and select options for including uppercase letters, lowercase letters, numbers, and special characters. We'll use standard Android UI components such as EditText for input fields and CheckBox for options. Additionally, we'll add a Button to trigger the password generation process and display the generated password to the user.

Code Implementation:

Now, let's go through the code implementation for each step:

Step 1: Designing the App

```kotlin
// Define password criteria
val minLength = 8
val includeUppercase = true
val includeLowercase = true
val includeNumbers = true
val includeSpecialCharacters = true
```

Step 2: Generating Random Characters

```kotlin
fun generateRandomCharacter(): Char {
    val charset = mutableListOf<Char>()
```

```
    if (includeUppercase) charset.addAll('A'..'Z')

    if (includeLowercase) charset.addAll('a'..'z')

    if (includeNumbers) charset.addAll('0'..'9')

    if    (includeSpecialCharacters)    charset.addAll("!@$%^&()_+-
=[]|,.<>?".toList())

    return charset.random()

}
```

Step 3: Building the User Interface

```xml
<!-- activity_main.xml -->

<LinearLayout ...>

  <EditText

    android:id="@+id/passwordLengthEditText"

    android:hint="Password Length"

    ... />

  <CheckBox

    android:id="@+id/uppercaseCheckBox"

    android:text="Include Uppercase Letters"

    ... />
```

```
    <!-- Add CheckBoxes for lowercase, numbers, and special
characters -->
    <Button
        android:id="@+id/generateButton"
        android:text="Generate Password"
        ... />
    <TextView
        android:id="@+id/passwordTextView"
        ... />
</LinearLayout>
```

```kotlin
// MainActivity.kt
class MainActivity : AppCompatActivity() {
    override fun onCreate(savedInstanceState: Bundle?) {
        super.onCreate(savedInstanceState)
        setContentView(R.layout.activity_main)

        val                    generateButton                    =
findViewById<Button>(R.id.generateButton)
```

153

```kotlin
    val                    passwordTextView               =
findViewById<TextView>(R.id.passwordTextView)


    generateButton.setOnClickListener {
        val                    passwordLength               =
passwordLengthEditText.text.toString().toInt()
        val password = generatePassword(passwordLength)
        passwordTextView.text = password
    }
}


private fun generatePassword(length: Int): String {
    val password = StringBuilder()
    repeat(length) {
        password.append(generateRandomCharacter())
    }
    return password.toString()
}
}
```

By following these steps and implementing the provided code snippets, we've successfully built a Password Generator App in Kotlin. The app allows users to specify the length of the password and select options for including uppercase letters, lowercase letters, numbers, and special characters. It then generates a random password based on the user's criteria and displays it to the user. This project demonstrates how to leverage Kotlin's features and Android's UI components to create a practical and functional app.

Chapter 9:
Understanding Classes and Objects

This chapter introduces the fundamental concepts of object-oriented programming in Kotlin. We'll delve into the creation of classes (blueprints for objects) and explore how objects encapsulate data and behavior. By the end, you'll be able to design reusable and modular code structures for your applications.

9.1: Introduction to Classes and Objects:

Imagine you're building a house. You wouldn't start by hammering random pieces of wood together. Instead, you'd have a blueprint - a detailed plan outlining the structure, rooms, and features of the house. In the world of programming, classes work similarly.

Classes as Blueprints:

 A class is a blueprint that defines the structure and behavior of a specific kind of object in your program.

 It acts as a template, specifying what properties (data) an object will have and what methods (functions) it can perform.

Think of it like this:

A class is like a recipe for a cake. It defines the ingredients (properties) like flour, sugar, and eggs. It also outlines the steps (methods) like mixing, baking, and cooling.

Just like following a recipe can create many delicious cakes, a class allows you to create multiple objects with the same structure and behavior.

Objects - Bringing the Blueprint to Life:

An object is an instance of a class. It's like a single cake baked from the recipe (class).

Each object has its own set of properties (data values) that may differ from other objects of the same class. For example, one cake might be a chocolate cake with chocolate frosting, while another might be a vanilla cake with strawberry filling.

Objects can also perform actions defined by the class methods. Continuing the cake analogy, both cakes can be sliced and eaten (methods).

Notes

A class defines the general structure and behavior, while objects are specific instances with their own data values.

You can create many objects from a single class, each with unique properties but sharing the same set of methods.

This concept of classes and objects is fundamental for building well-organized and reusable code in your Android applications.

9.2: Member Functions and Properties:

In object-oriented programming (OOP), a class serves as a blueprint for creating objects. These objects represent real-world entities or concepts with properties (data) and functionalities (methods) that manipulate that data. Here, we'll delve into member functions and properties, the essential components of a class.

9.2.1: Member Properties (Variables): Storing Object Data

Member properties (also known as member variables) are essentially variables attached to a class definition. They store data specific to each instance (object) created from that class.

Example:

```kotlin
class Person(val name: String, var age: Int) {

    // ... other member functions and properties

}
```

In the above example, `Person` is a class. It defines two member properties:

`name`: Stores the person's name as a string (set during object creation using `val`).

158

`age`: Stores the person's age as an integer (can be modified using `var`).

When you create objects (instances) of the `Person` class, each object will have its own copy of these properties with unique values.

9.2.2: Member Functions (Methods): Defining Object Behavior

Member functions (also known as methods) are blocks of code defined within a class. They define the functionalities (actions or behaviors) that an object can perform. These functions can operate on the object's data (member properties) or interact with other objects.

Example:

```kotlin
class Person(val name: String, var age: Int) {
    fun greet() {
        println("Hello, my name is $name and I am $age years old!")
    }

    fun increaseAge() {
        age++ // Modifies the object's age property
    }
}
```

```
```

Here, the `Person` class defines two member functions:

`greet()`: This function prints a greeting message using the object's `name` and `age` properties.

`increaseAge()`: This function increments the object's `age` property.

9.2.3: Access Modifiers: Controlling Property and Method Visibility

Access modifiers are keywords that define the accessibility of member properties and functions within a class and its subclasses. They control who (other code) can access and modify these members.

Common access modifiers:

public: Members are accessible from anywhere in your code.

private: Members are only accessible within the class itself.

protected: Members are accessible within the class and its subclasses (useful for inheritance).

Example:

```kotlin
class Person(val name: String, private var age: Int) {
    fun greet() { // Public function, accessible from anywhere
        println("Hello, my name is $name!")
```

```
    }


    private fun increaseAge() { // Private function, only accessible
within Person class

        age++

    }


    fun haveBirthday() { // Public function

        increaseAge() // Can call private function from within the class

    }
}
```

From this particular example:

    `name` is `public`, allowing access from anywhere in your code.

    `age` is `private`, restricting access to within the `Person` class.

    `greet()` is `public`, allowing you to call it to display the name.

    `increaseAge()` is `private`, but the `haveBirthday()` function
(public) can call it internally to modify the `age`.

Member properties and functions are the fundamental building blocks of objects in Kotlin.

By effectively using properties and methods, you can create objects that encapsulate data and behavior, leading to well-organized and maintainable code.

Access modifiers provide control over data integrity and promote code reusability.

9.3: Project 9: Building a Profile Management App:

Objective:

Design a `Profile` class to represent user information.

Implement functionalities to create, manage, and display user profiles.

Step 1: Designing the Profile Class

The `Profile` class will act as a blueprint for defining user profiles within your app. It will encapsulate the user's data and provide methods to access and modify that data.

```kotlin
class Profile(val name: String, val email: String, val picturePath: String) {
```

```
    // Additional methods can be defined here...


}
```
```

Explanation:

This class defines three properties:

`name`: A string representing the user's name.

`email`: A string representing the user's email address.

`picturePath`: A string representing the path to the user's profile picture (or a default image path if not provided).

The constructor takes these three arguments to initialize a new `Profile` object.

**Additional Methods (Optional):**

You can further enhance the `Profile` class by defining methods for:

`getFullName()`: To return the user's full name in a formatted way (e.g., including title or middle name).

`setPicture(newPath: String)`: To update the profile picture path when a new image is chosen.

`toString()`: To provide a string representation of the profile information for debugging or logging purposes.
```

Step 2: Creating and Managing Profiles

Now, let's build functionalities to handle profile creation, access, and modification:

1. Creating a Profile:

```kotlin
fun createProfile(name: String, email: String, picturePath: String): Profile {
    val newProfile = Profile(name, email, picturePath)
    // Add the new profile to a data store (implementation depends on chosen method)
    return newProfile
}
```

This function takes user-provided information and creates a new `Profile` object.

You'll need to implement logic to store the newly created profile object in a suitable data store. This could be:

A simple in-memory list (for demonstration purposes).

SharedPreferences for basic persistence across app sessions.

A Room database for more robust and scalable data storage.

2. Accessing Profile Information:

```kotlin
fun getProfile(name: String): Profile? {

    // Search for the profile in the data store based on name (or other identifier)

    // ... (implementation based on your chosen data store)

    // If found, return the Profile object, otherwise return null

}
```

This function allows retrieving an existing profile based on a search criteria (e.g., username).

The implementation will vary depending on your chosen data storage method.

3. Modifying Profile Information:

```kotlin
fun updateProfile(profile: Profile, newName: String?, newEmail: String?): Profile {

    val updatedProfile = profile.copy(

        name = newName ?: profile.name, // Use new name if provided, otherwise keep existing name
```

```
    email = newEmail ?: profile.email   // Similar logic for email
update

    )

    // Update the profile information in the data store

    // ... (implementation based on your chosen data store)

    return updatedProfile

}
```
```

This function allows updating an existing profile with new information (e.g., name or email).

It utilizes the `copy()` function to create a new `Profile` object with the modified properties while preserving the rest of the information.

Similar to profile creation, you'll need to update the data store with the changes.

**Step 3: Displaying User Profiles**

This step involves designing a user interface (UI) to showcase the user profile information in a visually appealing way. Here's a general outline:

**1. Create a Layout:**
```

- Design a layout using XML that includes elements to display the profile picture (ImageView), user name (TextView), email address (TextView), and potentially edit buttons for modifying the profile.

2. Populate the Layout with Profile Data:

- In your activity or fragment code, retrieve a user profile using the `getProfile()` function.

- Use the retrieved `Profile` object to set the content of the UI elements:

Set the `ImageView` source to the profile picture path.

Set the text of the `TextView`s for name and email using the corresponding properties from the `Profile` object.

Alternative 2

Project 9: Building a Profile Management App

Step 1: Designing the Profile Class

In this step, we'll define the properties and methods needed to represent user profiles. The Profile class will encapsulate information about each user, including their name, email, and profile picture.

```kotlin
class Profile(
    var name: String,
    var email: String,
```

```kotlin
    var profilePictureUrl: String
) {

    // Additional methods can be added here, such as methods for
updating profile information

}
```

In this code snippet, we define a Profile class with three properties: `name`, `email`, and `profilePictureUrl`. These properties represent the basic information associated with each user's profile. We can add additional methods to the Profile class as needed, such as methods for updating profile information.

Step 2: Creating and Managing Profiles

In this step, we'll implement logic to create new profiles, access and modify profile information, and potentially store profiles persistently. We'll create a ProfileManager class to handle these operations.

```kotlin
class ProfileManager {
    private val profiles = mutableListOf<Profile>()


    fun createProfile(name: String, email: String, profilePictureUrl:
String) {
```

```kotlin
        val profile = Profile(name, email, profilePictureUrl)

        profiles.add(profile)

    }


    fun getProfile(email: String): Profile? {

        return profiles.find { it.email == email }

    }


    fun updateProfile(email: String, newName: String,
newProfilePictureUrl: String) {

        val profile = profiles.find { it.email == email }

        profile?.apply {

            name = newName

            profilePictureUrl = newProfilePictureUrl

        }

    }

}
```

In this code snippet, we define a ProfileManager class with methods for creating, accessing, and updating profiles. We use a MutableList to store profiles, allowing us to add, remove, and modify profiles as needed.

Step 3: Displaying User Profiles

In this step, we'll design a user interface that displays profile information in a visually appealing manner. We'll use XML layouts to create the UI components, such as TextViews and ImageViews, and populate them with profile data.

```xml
<!-- profile_item.xml -->
<LinearLayout
xmlns:android="http://schemas.android.com/apk/res/android"
    android:layout_width="match_parent"
    android:layout_height="wrap_content"
    android:orientation="horizontal"
    android:padding="16dp">

    <ImageView
        android:id="@+id/profileImageView"
        android:layout_width="48dp"
        android:layout_height="48dp"
        android:src="@drawable/default_profile_picture"
        android:contentDescription="@string/profile_picture" />
```

```xml
<LinearLayout
    android:layout_width="0dp"
    android:layout_height="wrap_content"
    android:layout_weight="1"
    android:orientation="vertical"
    android:layout_marginStart="16dp">

    <TextView
        android:id="@+id/nameTextView"
        android:layout_width="wrap_content"
        android:layout_height="wrap_content"
        android:textSize="18sp"
        android:textColor="@color/black"
        android:textStyle="bold"
        android:text="Name" />

    <TextView
        android:id="@+id/emailTextView"
        android:layout_width="wrap_content"
        android:layout_height="wrap_content"
```

```
        android:textSize="16sp"

        android:textColor="@color/dark_gray"

        android:text="Email" />



    </LinearLayout>


</LinearLayout>
```

In this XML layout file (`profile_item.xml`), we define the layout for displaying a single user profile. It consists of an ImageView for the profile picture, along with TextViews for displaying the user's name and email.

In this project, we've created a profile management app using Kotlin. We designed the Profile class to represent user profiles, implemented logic for creating and managing profiles using the ProfileManager class, and designed a user interface to display profile information. By following these steps, we've built a functional app that allows users to create, access, and modify their profiles with ease.

Chapter 10:
Inheritance and Polymorphism

This chapter builds upon object-oriented programming by exploring inheritance and polymorphism. We'll learn how classes can inherit properties and methods from other classes, allowing for code reusability and creating more complex relationships between objects.

10.1: Understanding Inheritance:

Inheritance is a fundamental concept in object-oriented programming that allows you to create new classes (subclasses) based on existing classes (parent classes). It's like inheriting traits from your parents in real life! In code, inheritance promotes code reusability and simplifies the development process.

Key Concepts:

Class: A blueprint that defines the properties (attributes) and functionalities (methods) of an object. Think of a class as a template for creating objects.

Inheritance: The process of creating a new class (subclass) that inherits properties and methods from an existing class (parent class). The subclass becomes a more specialized version of the parent class.

Subclass (Child Class): A class that inherits from a parent class. It can access and use the inherited properties and methods from the parent.

Parent Class (Super Class): The class from which a subclass inherits properties and methods.

173

Benefits of Inheritance:

➢ Code Reusability: By inheriting properties and methods from a parent class, you avoid duplicating code. This saves development time and reduces the chances of errors.
➢ Extensibility: Subclasses can extend the functionality of the parent class by adding new methods or overriding inherited methods. This allows for specialization and customization.
➢ Hierarchical Relationships: Inheritance creates a hierarchy of classes, where more specialized classes inherit from more general ones. This helps organize your code and makes it easier to understand.

How Inheritance Works:

1. Define a Parent Class: You create a class that defines the common properties and functionalities that will be inherited by its subclasses.

2. Create a Subclass: You create a new class that inherits from the parent class. The subclass can:

UseInherited Properties and Methods: The subclass has direct access to the public and protected properties and methods defined in the parent class.

Override Inherited Methods: The subclass can redefine the behavior of an inherited method to provide its own specialized implementation.

Add New Properties and Methods: The subclass can introduce its own unique properties and methods that are specific to its functionality.

Example:

Imagine you're creating a mobile game with different characters. You can define a parent class `GameCharacter` with properties like `name`, `health`, and `attack()` method. Then, you can create subclasses like `Warrior` and `Archer` that inherit from `GameCharacter`. These subclasses can inherit the basic properties and `attack()` method, and also add their own unique properties and methods like `weapon` for Warrior or `rangedAttack()` for Archer.

10.2: Polymorphism: Treating Objects Differently:

Polymorphism is a fundamental concept in object-oriented programming (OOP) that allows objects of different classes to be treated in a similar way. It promotes code flexibility and reusability by enabling you to write code that works with a variety of related objects without needing to know their specific details.

Assuming you have a kennel that houses different types of animals: dogs, cats, birds, etc.

Each animal makes a different sound (woof, meow, chirp, etc.).

You want to create a function to make each animal speak.

Without polymorphism:

You would need to write separate functions for each animal type: `makeDogSpeak()`, `makeCatSpeak()`, `makeBirdSpeak()`, and so on.

This code would be repetitive and difficult to maintain, especially if you add new animal types later.

With polymorphism:

1. Create a base class called `Animal`:

This class can define common properties or functionalities that all animals share.

2. Define a method called `makeSound()` in the `Animal` class:

This method might be declared abstract (meaning it has no implementation in the base class), forcing subclasses to provide their own implementation.

3. Create subclasses for each animal type (Dog, Cat, Bird) that inherit from `Animal`:

These subclasses can override the `makeSound()` method to provide the specific sound each animal makes.

4. Create a function called `makeAnimalSpeak()` that takes an `Animal` object as a parameter:

This function can call the `makeSound()` method on the `Animal` object. Since it's a virtual function (abstract or overridden), the actual implementation called will depend on the specific animal object passed in (Dog, Cat, Bird).

Benefits of Polymorphism:

➤ Flexibility: You can write code that works with various animal objects without modifying the `makeAnimalSpeak()` function.
➤ Reusability: The `makeAnimalSpeak()` function can be reused for any new animal subclass you create in the future.
➤ Maintainability: The code is easier to understand and maintain because you avoid repetitive logic for each animal type.

Key Points:

Polymorphism allows objects of different classes (but with a common base class) to respond differently to the same method call.

Inheritance is a core concept that enables polymorphism by creating relationships between classes.

By using polymorphism, your code becomes more adaptable and easier to manage as your application grows.

In essence, polymorphism lets you treat different objects in a similar way, making your code more flexible and responsive to various situations.

10.3: Project 10: Building a Shape Calculator App:

In Project 10, we'll create a Shape Calculator app using Kotlin. This app will utilize inheritance and polymorphism to handle various shapes, allowing users to calculate the area and perimeter of different geometric shapes such as squares, circles, and rectangles.

Step 1: Designing Shape Classes

To start, we'll define abstract classes or interfaces for different shapes. These shape classes will have common properties like area and perimeter, which will be implemented by specific shape subclasses. Here's an example of how we can design the shape classes:

```kotlin
abstract class Shape {

    abstract fun area(): Double

    abstract fun perimeter(): Double

}


class Square(private val sideLength: Double) : Shape() {

    override fun area(): Double {

        return sideLength  sideLength

    }


    override fun perimeter(): Double {

        return 4  sideLength

    }
```

```
}

class Circle(private val radius: Double) : Shape() {

    override fun area(): Double {

        return Math.PI  radius  radius

    }


    override fun perimeter(): Double {

        return 2  Math.PI  radius

    }
}
```

In this example, we define an abstract class `Shape` with abstract functions `area()` and `perimeter()`. We then create concrete subclasses `Square` and `Circle`, each implementing their own calculation logic for area and perimeter.

Step 2: Implementing Specific Shapes

Next, we'll implement specific shape subclasses for other shapes like rectangles or triangles. We'll follow a similar pattern as above, defining properties and calculation logic for each shape.

Step 3: Building the Calculator

Finally, we'll design the user interface for the Shape Calculator app. We'll create an interface that allows users to choose a shape, input dimensions, and displays the calculated area or perimeter based on their selections. Here's a simplified version of how the interface might look:

```kotlin
fun main() {
    val square = Square(5.0)
    val circle = Circle(3.0)

    println("Square - Area: ${square.area()}, Perimeter: ${square.perimeter()}")
    println("Circle - Area: ${circle.area()}, Circumference: ${circle.perimeter()}")
}
```

In this example, we create instances of `Square` and `Circle`, passing in the required dimensions. We then print out the calculated area and perimeter for each shape.

Chapter 11:
Arrays and Collections: Efficient Data Management

This chapter introduces efficient ways to manage collections of data using arrays and collections like lists. We'll explore different collection types, adding, removing, iterating, and manipulating elements within these structures. By the end, you'll be able to organize and access large datasets effectively in your apps.

11.1: Understanding Arrays:

In programming, arrays are a fundamental data structure used to store collections of elements. They offer a powerful way to organize and manage similar types of data efficiently.

Key Concepts:

 Array: An array is a fixed-size, ordered collection of items all belonging to the same data type. Imagine it as a container with a set number of slots, each holding a single value.

 Data Type: The data type defines the kind of information an array can store. For example, an array can hold integers, floating-point numbers, strings, or even custom objects (depending on the programming language).

 Fixed Size: Unlike some other data structures, arrays have a predefined size that cannot be changed after creation. You need to determine the number of elements the array can hold upfront.

Indexing: Each element within an array has a unique identifier called its index. Indexing starts from 0 (zero) and goes up to the last element's index, which is one less than the size of the array. You use this index to access and manipulate individual elements.

Creating Arrays:

Here's a general approach to creating an array in many programming languages (including Kotlin):

1. Specify the data type: Declare the type of data the array will hold (e.g., integers, strings).

2. Define the size: Specify the number of elements the array can store.

3. Initialize (optional): You can optionally assign values to the elements during creation.

Example in Kotlin:

```kotlin
// Array to store temperatures (data type: integer)
val temperatures = IntArray(5) // Array with size 5 (can hold 5 integers)


// Initialize elements with specific values
temperatures[0] = 20 // Set the first element (index 0) to 20
temperatures[1] = 25 // Set the second element (index 1) to 25
```

// ... and so on for other elements

```

## Accessing Elements:

Once you have an array, you can access individual elements using their index within square brackets `[]`.

```kotlin

val firstTemperature = temperatures[0] // Access the value at index 0 (20 in this case)

```

Modifying Elements:

You can also modify the value of an element by assigning a new value to its index.

```kotlin

temperatures[2] = 18 // Change the value at index 2 to 18

```

 It's important to stay within the valid index range (0 to size-1) when accessing or modifying elements. Trying to access an index outside the bounds of the array will result in an error.
```

Arrays offer a simple and efficient way to manage similar data. They are particularly useful when you know the exact number of items you need to store beforehand.

11.2: Exploring Collections: Lists and More:

In programming, collections are like containers that hold multiple values in an organized way. While arrays are a fundamental data structure, they have limitations. In this chapter, we'll focus on lists, a powerful type of collection that offers more flexibility than arrays.

Why Use Lists?

❖ Dynamic Resizing: Unlike arrays with a fixed size, lists can grow or shrink as needed. You don't have to predetermine the number of elements you want to store.
❖ Heterogeneous Elements: Lists can hold elements of different data types within the same collection. This provides greater flexibility compared to arrays, which can only store elements of the same type.

Introducing Lists in Kotlin

Kotlin offers two main types of lists:

1. Mutable Lists: These lists allow you to add, remove, and modify elements after the list is created. They are ideal for situations where the data might change.

2. Immutable Lists: These lists are fixed in size and content after creation. They are useful for scenarios where data integrity is crucial, and you don't want accidental modifications.

Here, we'll focus on mutable lists, commonly used for dynamic data manipulation.

The most common way to create a mutable list in Kotlin is to use the `mutableListOf()` function:

```kotlin
val shoppingList = mutableListOf<String>("Milk", "Bread", "Eggs")
```

This code creates a mutable list named `shoppingList` that can hold elements of type `String`. The initial elements "Milk", "Bread", and "Eggs" are added to the list during creation.

Working with Lists: Adding, Removing, and More

Lists provide various methods for managing their elements:

Adding Elements:

`add(element)`: Appends the specified element to the end of the list.

`addAll(collection)`: Adds all elements from another collection to the end of the list.

`add(index, element)`: Inserts an element at a specific position (index) within the list.

Removing Elements:

`remove(element)`: Removes the first occurrence of the specified element from the list.

`removeAt(index)`: Removes the element at the specified index from the list.

`removeAll(collection)`: Removes all elements from the list that are also present in another collection.

Searching Elements:

`indexOf(element)`: Returns the index of the first occurrence of the specified element in the list, or -1 if not found.

`contains(element)`: Checks if the list contains the specified element and returns true or false.

Iterating through Elements:

You can use a `for` loop to iterate through each element in the list:

```kotlin
for (item in shoppingList) {
  println(item) // Prints each item in the shopping list
```

```
}
```
```
```

There are also other methods for iterating through lists with more advanced functionalities, but the `for` loop provides a simple way to access elements one by one.

Exploring Other Collections

Kotlin offers various collection types besides lists. Here are two common ones:

- Sets: Sets store unique elements and don't allow duplicates. They are useful for situations where you only need to keep track of distinct values.
- Maps: Maps store key-value pairs, similar to dictionaries in other languages. They allow you to associate unique keys with corresponding values.

By understanding and using lists effectively, you can manage dynamic data sets in your Kotlin programs. Lists provide a powerful foundation for building applications that require storing and manipulating collections of information.

Master the basic operations like adding, removing, searching, and iterating through elements to efficiently manage your lists.

Explore other collection types like sets and maps as your programming needs evolve.

By effectively utilizing collections, you'll be well-equipped to handle various data storage and manipulation scenarios within your Kotlin applications.

11.3: Project 11: Building a Shopping List App:

In this project, we'll create a simple shopping list app using Kotlin. The app will utilize lists to manage shopping list items, allowing users to add, remove, and mark items as purchased. Let's break down the steps needed to build the app.

Step 1: Designing the List Class

The first step is to define a class to represent shopping list items. Each item will have properties such as name, quantity, and whether it's checked off. Here's how we can define the List class:

```kotlin
class ListItem(val name: String, var quantity: Int, var isChecked: Boolean = false)
```

In this class, we define three properties: `name` (the name of the item), `quantity` (the quantity of the item), and `isChecked` (a boolean flag indicating whether the item is checked off).

Step 2: Managing the Shopping List

Next, we need to implement logic to add, remove, and mark items as purchased within the list. We'll create a ShoppingList class to manage these operations:

```kotlin
class ShoppingList {
    private val items = mutableListOf<ListItem>()

    fun addItem(item: ListItem) {
        items.add(item)
    }

    fun removeItem(item: ListItem) {
        items.remove(item)
    }

    fun markItemAsChecked(item: ListItem) {
        item.isChecked = true
    }
```

```kotlin
    fun markItemAsUnchecked(item: ListItem) {

        item.isChecked = false

    }

}
```

In this class, we use a mutable list to store the shopping list items. We define functions to add, remove, and mark items as checked or unchecked.

Step 3: Displaying the List

Finally, we need to design an interface that displays the shopping list items with checkboxes and allows adding or removing items. We'll create a simple console-based interface for demonstration purposes:

```kotlin
fun main() {

    val shoppingList = ShoppingList()

    // Adding items to the list

    shoppingList.addItem(ListItem("Apples", 5))

    shoppingList.addItem(ListItem("Bananas", 3))
```

```kotlin
shoppingList.addItem(ListItem("Milk", 1))

// Marking an item as checked
shoppingList.markItemAsChecked(shoppingList.items[0])

// Removing an item from the list
shoppingList.removeItem(shoppingList.items[1])

// Displaying the list
println("Shopping List:")
shoppingList.items.forEach { item ->
    val status = if (item.isChecked) " (Purchased)" else ""
    println("${item.name} - ${item.quantity}$status")
}
}
```

In this code, we create a ShoppingList instance and add some items to it. We then mark one item as purchased and remove another item from the list. Finally, we display the remaining items in the shopping list along with their quantities and purchase status.

In this project, we've built a simple shopping list app using Kotlin. We defined a List class to represent shopping list items, implemented logic to manage the shopping list, and designed a basic interface to display and interact with the list. This project demonstrates how to utilize lists to create practical applications and showcases the versatility of Kotlin as a programming language.

Chapter 12:
Working with Null Safety in Kotlin

This chapter delves into a crucial aspect of Kotlin: null safety. We'll understand how Kotlin helps avoid null pointer exceptions, common errors in programming, by ensuring variables are not accessed when they might be null.

12.1: Understanding Null Values and Null Safety:

In any programming language, variables can store data. But sometimes, a variable might not have a valid value assigned to it. This absence of a value is represented by a special concept called a null value.

1.1. What are Null Values?

Think of a null value as an empty box on a shelf. The box itself exists, but it doesn't contain anything. Similarly, a variable with a null value exists in your code, but it doesn't hold any actual data.

1.2. Why are Null Values Problematic?

While null values seem harmless initially, they can lead to unexpected behavior and crashes in your application. Imagine trying to use an object stored in a null variable – it's like trying to use an empty box! This can cause errors and crashes during program execution.

1.3. Introducing Null Safety in Kotlin

Kotlin, unlike some other programming languages, takes a stricter approach to handling null values. This approach is called null safety. Null safety helps prevent errors caused by accidentally using null values.

Kotlin achieves null safety through two main mechanisms:

Non-nullable types: By default, variables in Kotlin are declared with non-nullable types. This means they must always hold a valid value. You can't assign a null value to a non-nullable variable.

Nullable types: If you know a variable might legitimately be empty at some point, you can declare it with a nullable type. This is indicated by adding a question mark (`?`) after the data type. For example, `String?` represents a String variable that can be either a String value or null.

1.4. Working with Null Values in Kotlin:

To safely work with null values in Kotlin, you have special operators and techniques:

Null checks: Before using a variable that might be null, you can explicitly check if it contains a value using the `!= null` operator. This ensures you don't try to use an empty box.

Safe calls: The safe call operator (`?.`) allows you to access properties or call methods on a nullable variable only if it actually has a value. If the variable is null, the safe call operator simply returns null, preventing errors.

Elvis operator (`?:`) : This operator provides a default value if a nullable variable is null. It's a shorthand way to avoid long null checks and conditional statements.

1.5. Benefits of Null Safety:
By enforcing null safety, Kotlin helps you write more robust and reliable applications. It reduces the chances of crashes caused by null pointer exceptions, a common error in programming. Additionally, null safety improves code readability and maintainability by making it clear when a variable can be null or not.

Null values still exist in Kotlin, but null safety helps you manage them effectively, preventing errors and making your code more predictable.

12.2: Working with Nullable and Non-Nullable Types:

In Kotlin, variables can hold different types of data, like numbers, text, or even objects. Understanding how to declare and work with these types is essential for writing safe and reliable applications. This section dives into two important concepts: non-nullable types and nullable types.

12.2.1: Non-Nullable Types - Guaranteeing Data Presence

Non-nullable types: These types guarantee that a variable will always hold a valid value and cannot be null (absent).

Declaring non-nullable types: By default, Kotlin variables are non-nullable. You declare them simply by specifying the data type:

```kotlin
val name: String = "John Doe" // String is a non-nullable type

val age: Int = 30 // Int is also non-nullable


// Attempting to assign null to a non-nullable variable will result in a compilation error.

// val missingValue: String = null  // Error: Non-null type mismatch
```

Benefits of non-nullable types:

They improve code safety by preventing null pointer exceptions, which can crash your app.

They make your code more readable and clear about the expected data type.

12.2.2: Nullable Types - Handling Potential Absence of Data

Nullable types: These types allow a variable to hold a valid value or be null, indicating the absence of data.

Declaring nullable types: You use a question mark `?` after the data type to declare a nullable type:

```kotlin
var phoneNumber: String? = null // String? indicates a nullable String

var profileImage: Bitmap? = null   // Bitmap? indicates a nullable Bitmap
```

Benefits of nullable types:

They provide flexibility when dealing with data that might not always be available.

They prevent errors at compile time if a variable might be null initially.

12.2.3: Handling Nullable Types Safely

The Null Check Operator ("?") - The Preferred Approach:

When working with nullable types, you need to be cautious about accessing their properties or methods. Attempting to access a member (like a property or method) on a null variable will cause a null pointer exception.

Kotlin provides the null-check operator (`?`) to safely handle nullable types. It allows you to check if a variable is null before accessing its members:

```kotlin
fun greetUser(name: String?) {

    val message = name?.length // Checks if name is not null before accessing length

    if (message != null) {

        println("Hello, $name! Your name is $message characters long.")

    } else {

        println("Sorry, no name provided.")

    }

}
```

In this example:

`name?.length` checks if `name` is not null before accessing the `length` property.

198

If `name` is null, the expression evaluates to `null`.

The `if` statement handles both cases: null or a valid name.

The Not-Null Assertion Operator ("!!") - Use with Caution (Not Recommended for Beginners)

Kotlin also offers the not-null assertion operator (`!!`). It forces the evaluation of a nullable expression as non-null.

Warning: Using `!!` is risky! If the expression is actually null, it will result in a null pointer exception at runtime. This can lead to crashes and unexpected behavior in your app.

Recommendation: It's generally recommended to avoid `!!` and rely on the null-check operator (`?`) for safer code. The `?` operator helps you write code that is more robust and less prone to errors.

By understanding and effectively using non-nullable and nullable types, you can write cleaner, safer, and more reliable Kotlin code.

Always strive to use null checks (`?`) to handle nullable types and avoid potential null pointer exceptions.

Use `!!` with caution and only in very specific scenarios where you are absolutely certain the variable cannot be null.

12.3: Project 12: Building a Safe Note Taking App:

In this project, we'll build a safe note-taking app using Kotlin that prioritizes user privacy and security. We'll implement features to encrypt and store user notes securely, ensuring that sensitive information remains protected. By following each step and understanding the code provided, you'll learn how to incorporate encryption techniques into your Android applications, enhancing data security for your users.

Step 1: Setting Up Your Project

1. Open Android Studio and create a new project.

2. Choose a project name and select "Empty Activity" as the template.

3. Follow the prompts to set up your project, including choosing a package name and selecting your target API level.

Step 2: Designing the User Interface

1. Open the `activity_main.xml` layout file.

2. Design the layout to include a `EditText` for entering notes and a `Button` for saving notes.

Step 3: Adding Encryption Dependencies

1. Add the following dependency to your `build.gradle` file to use the Bouncy Castle library for encryption:

```groovy
```

implementation 'org.bouncycastle:bcpkix-jdk15on:1.68'

```
```

Step 4: Writing Kotlin Code

1. Open the `MainActivity.kt` file.

2. Import necessary packages:

```kotlin
import java.security.SecureRandom
import javax.crypto.Cipher
import javax.crypto.spec.IvParameterSpec
import javax.crypto.spec.SecretKeySpec
```

Step 5: Implementing Encryption Functions

1. Define functions for encryption and decryption:

```kotlin
fun encrypt(text: String, key: ByteArray): ByteArray {
    val cipher = Cipher.getInstance("AES/CBC/PKCS5Padding")
```

```kotlin
    val iv = ByteArray(cipher.blockSize)

    SecureRandom().nextBytes(iv)

    val ivParams = IvParameterSpec(iv)

    val secretKeySpec = SecretKeySpec(key, "AES")

    cipher.init(Cipher.ENCRYPT_MODE, secretKeySpec, ivParams)

    val encryptedText = cipher.doFinal(text.toByteArray())

    return iv + encryptedText
}


fun decrypt(encryptedText: ByteArray, key: ByteArray): String {
    val cipher = Cipher.getInstance("AES/CBC/PKCS5Padding")

    val iv = encryptedText.sliceArray(0 until cipher.blockSize)

    val ivParams = IvParameterSpec(iv)

    val secretKeySpec = SecretKeySpec(key, "AES")

    cipher.init(Cipher.DECRYPT_MODE, secretKeySpec, ivParams)

    val                       decryptedText                       =
cipher.doFinal(encryptedText.copyOfRange(cipher.blockSize,
encryptedText.size))

    return String(decryptedText)
}
```
```
```

Step 6: Implementing Note Saving and Retrieving

1. Implement functions to save and retrieve notes securely:

```kotlin
fun saveNote(note: String, key: ByteArray) {
    val encryptedNote = encrypt(note, key)
    // Save encryptedNote to SharedPreferences or other storage mechanism
}


fun retrieveNote(key: ByteArray): String? {
    // Retrieve encryptedNote from SharedPreferences or other storage mechanism
    // Decrypt encryptedNote using decrypt() function
    return decryptedNote
}
```

Step 7: Using the Functions in MainActivity

1. Use the `saveNote()` function to save the note when the user clicks the save button.

2. Use the `retrieveNote()` function to retrieve the note when the activity is created.

Step 8: Testing Your App

1. Run your app on an emulator or physical device.

2. Enter a note and click the save button.

3. Close and reopen the app to verify that the note is retrieved and displayed correctly.

Chapter 13:
Introduction to Android Development Concepts

This chapter provides a foundational understanding of core Android development concepts. We'll explore components like activities, views, and layouts, forming the building blocks of Android applications.

13.1: Understanding Activities and Layouts

In the world of Android app development, two fundamental concepts come together to create the user experience you see on screen: Activities and Layouts. Let's break down what each of these terms means and how they work together.

1. Activities: The Stages of Your App

Imagine your app as a play. An activity is like a single scene in that play. Each activity represents a specific screen or functionality within your app. It's where all the action happens – users interact with UI elements, data is displayed, and tasks are performed.

Here are some key points about activities:

 An app can have multiple activities, each with a distinct purpose. For example, you might have separate activities for a login screen, a home screen, and a settings screen.

Each activity has its own lifecycle, meaning it goes through stages like creation, being displayed on screen (resumed), paused (when another activity takes over), and finally destroyed when no longer needed.

You define the layout that belongs to each activity within an XML file. This layout file describes how the UI elements (buttons, text views, images, etc.) are arranged and displayed on the screen.

2. Layouts: The Blueprints for Your Screens

Think of a layout as the blueprint for your activity's screen. It's a structured design that defines how UI elements are positioned and organized. Layouts are written in XML, a simple and readable language specifically designed for describing user interfaces.

Here's what layouts do:

Layouts contain various UI elements like buttons, text views, images, and more.

Each element has its own properties that define its size, position, and visual appearance (color, font, etc.).

By combining different UI elements and their properties within a layout, you create the visual structure of your activity's screen.

Android offers different layout types like LinearLayout, RelativeLayout, and ConstraintLayout, each with its strengths for arranging elements in specific ways.

The Powerful Partnership: Activities and Layouts Working Together

Now comes the magic! Activities and layouts work hand-in-hand to bring your app to life:

An activity acts as a container, holding the layout that defines the screen's UI.

The layout tells the activity how to arrange and display the UI elements on the screen.

Together, they create the interactive experience users see and interact with when they use your app.

13.2: Exploring Views and User Interaction:

In the world of Android development, views are the fundamental building blocks that make up the visual element's users interact with on your app's screen. These elements can be anything from buttons and text fields for user input to image views for displaying pictures, text views for displaying information, and much more.

Understanding Views:

Views are like the building blocks of Legos – they come in various shapes and functionalities, allowing you to construct the user interface (UI) of your app.

Each view represents a single UI element with its own properties and behaviors.

By combining different types of views and arranging them strategically, you create the visual layout and functionality for your app's screens.

Types of Views:

Android offers a rich set of built-in views to cater to various UI needs. Here are some common types:

Button: A clickable element that triggers an action when pressed (e.g., starting a new activity, submitting data).

TextView: Displays text information on the screen. You can customize fonts, styles, and text alignment.

EditText: Allows users to enter text input, ideal for capturing user information like names, emails, or search queries.

ImageView: Displays images on the screen. You can load images from resources or dynamically from the internet.

LinearLayout: A layout manager that arranges views horizontally or vertically in a single row or column.

RelativeLayout: A layout manager that positions views relative to each other or the parent layout.

ConstraintLayout: A powerful layout manager offering flexible positioning options based on constraints between views.

Using Views in Your App:

1. Choosing the Right View:

- Identify the purpose of each UI element you want to create (e.g., displaying text, capturing user input, triggering actions).
- Select the appropriate view type based on the functionality you need.

2. Customizing Views with Properties:

- Each view type has various properties you can set to control its appearance and behavior.
- These properties can be defined in your layout resource files (XML) using attributes.
- For example, you can set the text displayed on a button using the `android:text` attribute, or change the background color of a view using the `android:background` attribute.

3. Arranging Views with Layouts:

- Views don't appear on the screen by themselves. You need to use layout managers to arrange them in a specific order and structure.
- Layout managers like LinearLayout, RelativeLayout, and ConstraintLayout help you define the positioning and organization of views within your app's screens.

Benefits of Using Views Effectively:

- o Reusable Components: Views are reusable building blocks, allowing you to create complex UI elements by combining simpler views.
- o Modular Design: By separating the UI logic from the app's core functionality, you can maintain a clean and organized codebase.
- o Flexibility: The wide variety of views and layout managers allows you to design user interfaces for any app concept.

13.3: Project 13: Building a Simple Greeting App (Android Version):

In this project, we'll build a basic Android app that allows users to input their name and receive a personalized greeting message. This app will provide a practical example of handling user input and displaying dynamic content in an Android application.

Step 1: Setting Up Your Project

1. Open Android Studio and create a new project.

2. Choose a project name and select "Empty Activity" as the template.

3. Follow the prompts to set up your project, including choosing a package name and selecting your target API level.

Step 2: Designing the User Interface

1. Open the activity_main.xml layout file.

2. Design the layout to include a TextView for displaying the greeting message and an EditText for users to input their name.

```xml
<RelativeLayout
xmlns:android="http://schemas.android.com/apk/res/android"
    xmlns:tools="http://schemas.android.com/tools"
```

```
android:layout_width="match_parent"

android:layout_height="match_parent"

tools:context=".MainActivity">


<EditText

    android:id="@+id/nameEditText"

    android:layout_width="match_parent"

    android:layout_height="wrap_content"

    android:hint="Enter your name"

    android:layout_marginTop="16dp"

    android:layout_centerHorizontal="true"/>


<Button

    android:id="@+id/greetButton"

    android:layout_width="wrap_content"

    android:layout_height="wrap_content"

    android:text="Greet"

    android:layout_below="@id/nameEditText"

    android:layout_centerHorizontal="true"

    android:layout_marginTop="16dp"/>
```

```
    <TextView

        android:id="@+id/greetingTextView"

        android:layout_width="wrap_content"

        android:layout_height="wrap_content"

        android:layout_below="@id/greetButton"

        android:layout_centerHorizontal="true"

        android:layout_marginTop="16dp"

        android:textSize="20sp"/>

</RelativeLayout>
```

Step 3: Writing Kotlin Code

1. Open the MainActivity.kt file.

2. Define variables to reference the EditText and TextView:

```kotlin
import android.os.Bundle

import android.widget.Button

import android.widget.EditText
```

```kotlin
import android.widget.TextView

import androidx.appcompat.app.AppCompatActivity


class MainActivity : AppCompatActivity() {
    override fun onCreate(savedInstanceState: Bundle?) {
        super.onCreate(savedInstanceState)
        setContentView(R.layout.activity_main)


        val nameEditText = findViewById<EditText>(R.id.nameEditText)
        val greetButton = findViewById<Button>(R.id.greetButton)
        val greetingTextView = findViewById<TextView>(R.id.greetingTextView)
    }
}
```

Step 4: Handling User Input and Displaying Greeting

1. Inside the `onCreate()` method, add a click listener to the greetButton:

```kotlin
greetButton.setOnClickListener {
```

```
    val name = nameEditText.text.toString()

    val greetingMessage = "Hello, $name!"

    greetingTextView.text = greetingMessage

}
```

Step 5: Testing Your App

1. Run your app on an emulator or physical device.

2. Enter your name into the EditText field and click the "Greet" button.

3. Observe the personalized greeting message displayed in the TextView.

Congratulations! You've successfully built a Simple Greeting App for Android. Users can input their name, and the app will greet them with a personalized message. This project demonstrates the basics of handling user input and updating the UI dynamically in an Android application.

Chapter 14:
Utilizing Resources and Adapting UI for Different Devices

This chapter introduces resources, essential for managing different elements like text, images, and styles within your app. Additionally, we'll explore techniques to adapt the user interface for various screen sizes and devices.

14.1: Working with Resources: Strings, Images, and Styles:

In Android app development, resources are essential building blocks that provide non-code assets for your application. These resources include elements like text, images, colors, styles, and more. Effectively managing resources helps to:

Separate code from data: Resources keep your code clean and maintainable by storing text, images, and other data outside of your core programming logic.

Localization: Resources allow you to easily adapt your app for different languages and regions by providing alternative versions of text content.

Theming: Resources enable you to define and apply consistent visual styles throughout your app, improving its overall look and feel.

215

Here's a breakdown of some key types of resources and how to use them in your Android apps:

1. Strings:

What are they? String resources store textual content displayed within your app, such as button labels, error messages, or UI text.

How to use them:

Create a file named `strings.xml` in your project's `res/values` directory.

Define string resources using key-value pairs within the XML file.

Access string resources in your code using the `getString(resource_id)` method, passing the resource ID (key) defined in the `strings.xml` file.

Example:
```xml
<resources>
  <string name="app_name">My Awesome App</string>
  <string name="button_label">Click Me!</string>
  <string name="error_message">An error occurred. Please try again.</string>
```

</resources>

```

```java
// Accessing string resources

String appName = getString(R.string.app_name);
```

2. Images:

What are they? Image resources store visual assets like icons, logos, or any other pictures used within your app.

How to use them:

Place image files (e.g., PNG, JPEG) in appropriate drawable resource folders based on their size and density (e.g., `drawable-mdpi`, `drawable-xhdpi`).

Reference images in your layout files using the `android:src` attribute of UI elements like `ImageView`.

Alternatively, access images in your code using `getDrawable(resource_id)`.

Example:
```xml

```xml
<ImageView

    android:id="@+id/app_icon"

    android:layout_width="wrap_content"

    android:layout_height="wrap_content"

    android:src="@drawable/app_icon" />
```

3. Styles:

What are they? Styles encapsulate a set of visual properties like text color, background color, text size, etc., allowing you to apply them consistently to various UI elements.

How to use them:

Create a style file named `styles.xml` in your project's `res/values` directory.

Define styles using XML tags, specifying properties like `textColor`, `textSize`, `backgroundColor`, etc.

Apply styles to UI elements in your layouts using the `android:style` attribute.

Example:

```xml
<resources>
```

```xml
    <style name="PrimaryButtonStyle">

        <item name="android:textColor">@color/white</item>

        <item
name="android:backgroundColor">@color/primary_color</item>

        <item name="android:textSize">16sp</item>

    </style>

</resources>


<Button

    android:id="@+id/primary_button"

    android:layout_width="wrap_content"

    android:layout_height="wrap_content"

    android:text="Click Me"

    android:style="@style/PrimaryButtonStyle" />  ```
```

Effectively utilizing resources promotes code organization, maintainability, and a consistent user experience in your Android applications.

Explore the Android documentation for a comprehensive list of available resource types and their usage guidelines.

14.2: Adapting UI for Different Screens:

14.2.1: Responsive Layouts with Relative Layout and Weights

Relative Layout: This layout positions elements relative to each other or the parent layout's edges. It's ideal for creating flexible UIs that can adjust to different screen sizes.

Imagine a simple layout with two buttons: one on the left and one on the right. Using a Relative Layout, you can define the positions of these buttons relative to each other (e.g., one to the left of the other) instead of specifying fixed pixel values. This ensures the buttons maintain their desired relative positions even when the screen size changes.

Weight Units: Relative Layout utilizes weight units to distribute available space proportionally between child elements. Imagine a layout with two buttons, and you want them to share the remaining space equally after accommodating other elements. By assigning a weight of 1 to each button, the layout will distribute the remaining horizontal space equally between them, making them appear side-by-side and automatically adjusting their sizes as the screen resizes.

Example:

```xml
<RelativeLayout
    android:layout_width="match_parent"
    android:layout_height="wrap_content">
```

```xml
    <Button

        android:id="@+id/button1"

        android:layout_width="wrap_content"

        android:layout_height="wrap_content"

        android:text="Button 1"

        android:layout_alignParentLeft="true"
android:layout_margin="8dp" />


    <Button

        android:id="@+id/button2"

        android:layout_width="wrap_content"

        android:layout_height="wrap_content"

        android:text="Button 2"

        android:layout_toRightOf="@+id/button1"
android:layout_alignParentRight="true"
android:layout_margin="8dp"  android:layout_weight="1" />


</RelativeLayout>
```
```
```

In this example, `button1` is positioned to the left of the parent layout with some margin. `button2` is placed to the right of `button1` and also aligned to the right edge of the parent layout. The weight of 1 assigned to `button2` ensures it takes up the remaining space proportionally. As the screen size changes, the buttons will adjust their sizes and positions while maintaining their relative placement.

14.2.2: Resource Qualifiers for Targeted Layouts

Resource Qualifiers: Android offers a mechanism called resource qualifiers to provide alternative layouts or resources based on device characteristics like screen size, orientation (portrait/landscape), language, and more.

Imagine you have a complex layout that looks great in portrait mode but might appear cluttered in landscape mode. Using resource qualifiers, you can create a separate layout specifically optimized for landscape orientation. When the device switches to landscape mode, Android will automatically load and use this alternative layout, ensuring an optimal user experience regardless of the screen orientation.

Implementing Resource Qualifiers: Resource qualifiers are denoted by suffixes appended to resource filenames. Here are some common examples:

`-sw600dp`: Indicates a screen width of at least 600dp (large screen).

`-land`: Indicates landscape orientation.

`-en`: Indicates English language.

By creating separate layout files with these qualifiers, you can provide targeted layouts for different screen sizes, orientations, and other device characteristics.

Example:

Create a folder named `layout-land` within your project's `res` directory.

Inside this folder, create a copy of your main layout file named with the `-land` qualifier (e.g., `activity_main.xml-land`).

In this alternative layout file, modify the layout structure or element positioning to optimize it for landscape orientation.

Now, when the device switches to landscape mode, Android will automatically load and use the layout file with the `-land` qualifier, providing a more suitable UI for the changed orientation.

14.3: Project 14: Building a Quote Viewer App:

In this project, we'll create a simple Quote Viewer App using Kotlin. The app will display a collection of quotes and allow users to view them one by one. This project will demonstrate how to load data from a list, display it in a user interface, and implement basic navigation functionality.

Step 1: Setting Up Your Project

1. Open Android Studio and create a new project.

2. Choose a project name and select "Empty Activity" as the template.

3. Follow the prompts to set up your project, including choosing a package name and selecting your target API level.

Step 2: Designing the User Interface

1. Open the activity_main.xml layout file.

2. Design the layout to include a TextView for displaying the quote and Buttons for navigating between quotes.

```xml
<?xml version="1.0" encoding="utf-8"?>
<RelativeLayout
xmlns:android="http://schemas.android.com/apk/res/android"
    xmlns:tools="http://schemas.android.com/tools"
    android:layout_width="match_parent"
    android:layout_height="match_parent"
    tools:context=".MainActivity">
```

```xml
<TextView
    android:id="@+id/quoteTextView"
    android:layout_width="wrap_content"
    android:layout_height="wrap_content"
    android:text="Quote will be displayed here"
    android:layout_centerInParent="true"
    android:textSize="20sp"
    android:textAlignment="center"/>

<Button
    android:id="@+id/prevButton"
    android:layout_width="wrap_content"
    android:layout_height="wrap_content"
    android:text="Previous"
    android:layout_alignParentStart="true"
    android:layout_alignParentBottom="true"
    android:layout_marginStart="16dp"
    android:layout_marginBottom="16dp"/>
```

```xml
    <Button

        android:id="@+id/nextButton"

        android:layout_width="wrap_content"

        android:layout_height="wrap_content"

        android:text="Next"

        android:layout_alignParentEnd="true"

        android:layout_alignParentBottom="true"

        android:layout_marginEnd="16dp"

        android:layout_marginBottom="16dp"/>


</RelativeLayout>
```

Step 3: Writing Kotlin Code

1. Open the MainActivity.kt file.

2. Define a list of quotes and an index to keep track of the current quote.

3. Initialize the TextView with the first quote from the list.

4. Implement functionality for the "Next" and "Previous" buttons to navigate through the quotes.

````kotlin
class MainActivity : AppCompatActivity() {
    private val quotes = listOf(
        "Be yourself; everyone else is already taken. - Oscar Wilde",
        "Two things are infinite: the universe and human stupidity; and I'm not sure about the universe. - Albert Einstein",
        "So many books, so little time. - Frank Zappa"
    )

    private var currentQuoteIndex = 0

    override fun onCreate(savedInstanceState: Bundle?) {
        super.onCreate(savedInstanceState)
        setContentView(R.layout.activity_main)

        displayCurrentQuote()

        findViewById<Button>(R.id.nextButton).setOnClickListener {
            if (currentQuoteIndex < quotes.size - 1) {
                currentQuoteIndex++
                displayCurrentQuote()
````

```
        }

    }


    findViewById<Button>(R.id.prevButton).setOnClickListener {
        if (currentQuoteIndex > 0) {
            currentQuoteIndex--
            displayCurrentQuote()
        }
    }
}


private fun displayCurrentQuote() {
    findViewById<TextView>(R.id.quoteTextView).text          =
quotes[currentQuoteIndex]
    }
}
```

Step 4: Testing Your App

1. Run your app on an emulator or physical device.

2. Click the "Next" button to navigate to the next quote.

3. Click the "Previous" button to navigate to the previous quote.

You've successfully built a Quote Viewer App using Kotlin. Users can now view a collection of quotes and navigate through them using simple button controls. This project demonstrates the basic principles of loading and displaying data in an Android app and provides a solid foundation for building more complex applications in the future.

Chapter 15:
Connecting Your App to the Outside World with APIs

This final chapter introduces the concept of APIs (Application Programming Interfaces). We'll discuss how APIs allow your app to communicate with external services and access data from various sources, enriching its functionalities.

15.1: Understanding APIs and their Purpose:

In the world of software development, APIs (Application Programming Interfaces) play a crucial role in enabling communication between different applications and services. Imagine them as waiters in a restaurant – they take your order (requests from your app) and deliver it to the kitchen (external service) and bring back the prepared food (response from the service).

What are APIs?

An API is essentially a set of rules and specifications that define how one application can interact with another application or service. It acts as a messenger, allowing your app to request information or functionality from an external source without needing to know the internal workings of that source.

Why are APIs Important?

APIs offer several advantages for developers:

- ✓ Simplified Development: Instead of building everything from scratch, APIs provide pre-built functionalities you can integrate into your app, saving time and effort.
- ✓ Access to External Data: APIs allow your app to access and utilize data from external sources like weather information, social media feeds, or online databases.
- ✓ Enhanced Functionality: By leveraging APIs from various services, you can extend the features and capabilities of your app beyond its core functionality.
- ✓ Improved User Experience: By incorporating functionalities like user authentication, payment processing, or location services through APIs, you can create a more convenient and feature-rich experience for your users.

Types of APIs:

There are various types of APIs, each serving a specific purpose:

1. Web APIs (REST APIs): These are the most common type, accessed over the internet using HTTP requests. They follow a well-defined architectural style called REST (Representational State Transfer) for data exchange.
2. Internal APIs: These APIs are designed for communication within a single organization or between different components within a large software system.
3. Mobile APIs: These APIs are specifically designed for use with mobile applications, often providing functionalities tailored to the mobile environment.

4. Database APIs: These APIs allow applications to interact with databases to store, retrieve, and manipulate data.

How APIs Work:

Here's a simplified breakdown of how APIs work:

1. Your App Makes a Request: Your app sends a request to the API using a specific format (often including the desired data or action).

2. API Processes the Request: The API receives and interprets the request, identifying the desired information or functionality.

3. API Fetches or Performs Actions: The API retrieves the requested data from its source (e.g., database) or performs the requested action (e.g., user authentication).

4. API Sends a Response: The API sends a response back to your app, containing the requested data, confirmation of the action, or any error messages if applicable.

5. Your App Handles the Response: Your app receives and interprets the response, using the information or acting upon the results accordingly.

Benefits for Both Developers and Users:

APIs offer a win-win situation for both developers and users:

Developers: They gain access to pre-built functionalities, saving development time and effort.

Users: They experience a more feature-rich and convenient app with functionalities powered by external APIs.

15.2: Making Simple API Calls in Kotlin:

In many Android applications, you'll interact with web servers to fetch or send data. This communication often involves API calls (Application Programming Interface). APIs provide a structured way for your app to access data and functionalities offered by external services.

This section introduces basic techniques for making API calls in Kotlin using popular libraries:

1. Understanding API Calls:

An API acts as a messenger between your app and a web server.

You make a request to the API specifying what data you need, and the server responds with the requested data or an appropriate message (e.g., success or error).

Data is often exchanged in a format like JSON (JavaScript Object Notation), a lightweight and human-readable way to represent structured data.

2. Popular Kotlin Libraries for API Calls:

Retrofit: A powerful and popular library for building type-safe and asynchronous API clients.

Volley: A simpler library by Google for making HTTP requests and handling responses.

3. Making an API Call with Retrofit (Example):

Here's a simplified example demonstrating the core concepts of making an API call using Retrofit:

3.1. Setting Up Retrofit:

Add the Retrofit library to your project's dependencies using Gradle.

Define an interface with methods annotated with `@GET`, `@POST`, `@PUT`, or `@DELETE` to specify the API endpoint and request type (Get, Post, Put, Delete).

Use the `@Url` annotation within the method to define the API endpoint URL.

```kotlin
interface ApiService {

    @GET("/users")

    suspend fun getUsers(): List<UserData> // Example API endpoint to get a list of users

}
```

3.2. Building the Retrofit Client:
Create a Retrofit client instance using the `Retrofit.Builder` class.

Specify the base URL of the API server you're interacting with.

Add an adapter to convert JSON responses to Kotlin objects (e.g., using Gson converter).

```kotlin
val retrofit = Retrofit.Builder()
    .baseUrl("https://api.example.com/")
    .addConverterFactory(GsonConverterFactory.create())
    .build()
```

3.3. Making the API Request:
Use the Retrofit client to create an instance of the API interface.

Call the desired method from the interface to initiate the API request.

Retrofit calls are asynchronous, meaning they run in the background without blocking the main thread.

```kotlin
val apiService = retrofit.create(ApiService::class.java)
```

```kotlin
val users = apiService.getUsers() // This is a suspend function
```

3.4. Handling the Response (asynchronously):
Since Retrofit calls are asynchronous, you need to use coroutines or a similar mechanism to handle the response in a non-blocking way.

Use `await()` or a coroutine scope to wait for the response and retrieve the data (or handle errors).

```kotlin
CoroutineScope(Dispatchers.IO).launch {

    try {

        val response = users.await() // Waits for the response asynchronously

        // Handle successful response and access the user data from 'response'

    } catch (e: Exception) {

        // Handle API call errors

    }

}
```

4. Key Points to Remember:

This is a simplified example. Real-world API calls might involve authentication, authorization headers, request parameters, and more complex response handling.

Retrofit offers more features like converter factories for different data formats and interceptor support for adding custom logic to requests and responses.

Volley provides a simpler approach but may lack some of the advanced features and type safety of Retrofit.

5. Next Steps:

Explore the detailed documentation of Retrofit or Volley for a comprehensive understanding of their functionalities and advanced usage patterns.

Practice making API calls to real-world APIs (with proper permissions or using public APIs) to solidify your understanding and gain experience with data fetching and interaction.

15.3: Project 15: Building a Weather App (using a Free Weather API):

In this project, we'll build a Weather App using a free Weather API. This app will allow users to retrieve weather information for a specific location by making requests to the API. We'll cover all the necessary steps and code needed to create the app, from setting up the project to displaying the weather data on the user interface.

Step 1: Setting Up Your Project

1. Open Android Studio and create a new project.

2. Choose a project name and select "Empty Activity" as the template.

3. Follow the prompts to set up your project, including choosing a package name and selecting your target API level.

Step 2: Adding Internet Permission

1. Open the AndroidManifest.xml file.

2. Add the following line inside the `<manifest>` tag to request permission to access the internet:

```xml
<uses-permission android:name="android.permission.INTERNET" />
```

Step 3: Adding Retrofit Dependency

1. Open the build.gradle (Module: app) file.

2. Add the Retrofit dependency inside the dependencies block:

```gradle
```

```
implementation 'com.squareup.retrofit2:retrofit:2.9.0'
```

Step 4: Creating Retrofit Interface

1. Create a new Kotlin interface called WeatherApiService.

2. Define a function to make a GET request to the Weather API:

```kotlin
interface WeatherApiService {
    @GET("weather")
    fun getWeather(
        @Query("q") location: String,
        @Query("appid") apiKey: String
    ): Call<WeatherResponse>
}
```

Step 5: Defining WeatherResponse Class

1. Create a new Kotlin data class called WeatherResponse.

2. Define properties to represent the weather data returned by the API:

```kotlin
```

```kotlin
data class WeatherResponse(
    val main: Main,
    val weather: List<Weather>
)

data class Main(
    val temp: Double,
    val humidity: Int
)

data class Weather(
    val description: String
)
```

Step 6: Implementing WeatherService

1. Create a new Kotlin class called WeatherService.

2. Implement a function to make a request to the Weather API using Retrofit:

```kotlin
object WeatherService {
```

```kotlin
    private            const        val          BASE_URL          =
"https://api.openweathermap.org/data/2.5/"

    private const val API_KEY = "your_api_key_here"


    private val retrofit = Retrofit.Builder()

        .baseUrl(BASE_URL)

        .addConverterFactory(GsonConverterFactory.create())

        .build()


    private                val                service              =
retrofit.create(WeatherApiService::class.java)


    fun getWeather(location: String): Call<WeatherResponse> {

        return service.getWeather(location, API_KEY)

    }

}
```

Step 7: Displaying Weather Data

1. Open the activity_main.xml layout file.

2. Design the layout to include TextViews to display temperature, humidity, and weather description.

Step 8: Updating MainActivity

1. Open the MainActivity.kt file.

2. Implement a function to fetch weather data and update the UI:

```kotlin
private fun fetchWeatherData(location: String) {

    WeatherService.getWeather(location).enqueue(object                    :
Callback<WeatherResponse> {

        override fun onResponse(

            call: Call<WeatherResponse>,

            response: Response<WeatherResponse>

        ) {

            if (response.isSuccessful) {

                val weatherResponse = response.body()

                val temperature = weatherResponse?.main?.temp

                val humidity = weatherResponse?.main?.humidity

                val                    description                    =
weatherResponse?.weather?.firstOrNull()?.description
```

```kotlin
            // Update UI with weather data

            temperatureTextView.text          =          "Temperature:
${temperature?.toString()}°C"

            humidityTextView.text          =          "Humidity:
${humidity?.toString()}%"

            descriptionTextView.text = "Description: $description"

        }

    }


    override  fun  onFailure(call:  Call<WeatherResponse>,  t:
Throwable) {

        // Handle failure

    }

  })

 }
```

3. Call the `fetchWeatherData()` function with the desired location
when needed.

Step 9: Testing Your App

243

1. Run your app on an emulator or physical device.

2. Enter a location (e.g., city name) and observe the weather data displayed on the UI.

Congratulations! You've successfully built a Weather App using a free Weather API. Users can now retrieve and view weather information for a specific location using your app. This project demonstrates how to integrate Retrofit to make network requests and handle API responses in an Android app.

Note: This outline does not provide specific code examples due to the potential for API changes and limitations. However, it provides a roadmap for the final project, enabling readers to research and explore specific APIs based on their chosen weather data provider.

By completing these 15 chapters and their corresponding projects, you'll gain a foundational understanding of Kotlin, essential concepts of Android development, and the capabilities to build basic Android apps that interact with the outside world through APIs. Remember, continued practice and exploration are key to further mastering your skills in this exciting domain.

www.ingramcontent.com/pod-product-compliance
Lightning Source LLC
Chambersburg PA
CBHW080638060326
40690CB00021B/4978